JEEP

JEEP

MICHAEL CLAYTON

David & Charles
Newton Abbot   London   North Pomfret (Vt)

British Library Cataloguing in Publication Data

Clayton, Michael
  Jeep.
   1. Jeep automobile
   I. Title
  623.74'722'09   TL215.J44
  ISBN 0-7153-8066-4

Photoset by Typesetters (Birmingham) Ltd,
and printed in Great Britain
by Butler & Tanner Ltd, Frome, Somerset
for David & Charles (Publishers) Limited
Brunel House Newton Abbot Devon

Published in the United States of America
by David & Charles Inc
North Pomfret Vermont 05053 USA

CONTENTS

1
ORIGINS

The Jeep in US Army insignia had been in front of mine for some hours when I fell asleep on the long run from Frankfurt to Berlin in 1945. I might have remained in ignorance of my brief lapse if the road ahead had not been empty when I woke up. I stopped. Walking back in the dark to investigate, I found it impossible to discern anything except that this section of road was elevated and had a frighteningly steep embankment dropping into pastures on the right. While I wondered how to scramble down, the tranquility of the night was broken by the roar of an engine, followed by the stab of headlights as the front wheels of the Jeep clawed over the lip of the road. The driver joined me for a brisk walk while we talked about the dangers of falling asleep at the wheel. But the capability of the Jeep to rejoin the road was taken for granted. Such was the serviceman's trust in the Jeep's ability.

So where did this vehicle acquire that touch of genius? Certainly not with one man or in one place. The need for a military vehicle of the go-anywhere type had been recognised on the appallingly muddy battlefields of World War I. Military innovators played their part as did civilians, some designs being based on the famous Ford Model T. It was in June 1940, with the introduction of a specification by the US Army, that the competition for the Jeep as we know it really took off. Yet, even then, in spite of an incredible 135 companies being invited to take up the challenge, only three competed: Bantam (formerly American Austin), Willys and Ford.

The last two names, particularly Willys, are synonymous with veteran Jeeps, but the Bantam name has disappeared without its full share of the glory. Originally the American Austin Car Co Inc of Butler, Pennsylvania, formed in 1930, it became the American Bantam Car Co Inc in 1935 and continued in car manufacture until 1941. The Austin name had no direct connection with the famous British company best known for the Austin Seven at that time. However, the Bantam car was, in fact, an Austin Seven produced under licence with mirror-image engine, and styling in the manner of a Chevrolet of the period. By 1937, with a body styled by Alexis de Sakhnoffski, it was a most attractive car, but a sub-compact did not appeal – even in 1940 when engine size increased to a still tiny swept volume of 800cc. In that same year, however, Bantam produced the first successful Jeep prototype with a 4-cylinder Continental engine. It saved the company but, as the Jeep story continued, Bantam finally dropped out of the automotive field.

The Jeep specification of the Ordnance Technical Committee in Washington DC went out on 27 June 1940. The day of the month was important as any manufacturer entering the 'competition' had to deliver 70 vehicles in 75 days. It was no wonder that of 135 manufacturers circularised only 3 responded. The demand was for a ¼-ton 4×4 truck, the 4×4 meaning that all 4 wheels were driven.

The specification listed basic demands including: a weight limit of 1,300lb (590kg) and a pay-load of 600lb (272kg); the engine had to develop 85ft (26m) lb (450g) torque; the wheelbase maximum was 80in (2m), and the maximum track (or tread in American terminology) was 47in (1.19m). Such was the urgency that the approach to 135 manufacturers was without precedent. Further, the first prototype had to be delivered within forty-nine days and the remainder within a period of twenty-six days — and this to include changes demanded by the Quartermaster's office.

For the sake of precision, it should be on record that only Bantam and Willys-Overland Motors were in at the start. However, Willys knew that it could not get axles in time and asked for 120 days. This was agreed, but only on the basis that there would be a penalty for each day over the original date at the rate (in the real values of the day) of $5. Meanwhile, Bantam took a chance on seventy-five days. Willys-Overland produced what seemed the cheaper answer, but its costings worked out higher than Bantam's because of the penalty clause.

Bantam won the order.

One man was outstanding in this Bantam victory — the late Karl K. Probst. This automotive consultant joined the American Bantam firm as chief engineer (temporary) in July 1940. The extraordinary factor is that he designed what in effect was to become the Jeep in five days, and masterminded building the prototype in forty-nine days. Involved with him were Roy S. Evans, Francis H. Feen, C. H. Payne and Harold Crist (of whom more later).

It was Roy Evans' later tenacity that resulted in a monument to the birth of the Jeep being erected in the company's home town of Butler, Pennsylvania. Most of the Bantams were destined under lend-lease to Great Britain and Russia. The serial numbers of the first 1,500 were 1072–2572 and had US registered numbers beginning with W-2015919. So few have survived that they are hungrily sought by collectors.

Bantam alone had to take the criticism, though, partly because it was the only target and also because the weight limit was so low. Col John

Every serviceman liked to be photographed with 'his' Jeep. These Press Unit RAF sergeants (Germany, 1946) were no exception. On the right Johnny Saunders; on the left Ron Easton, now chief photographer of *Autocar* magazine

H. Claybrook pointed out that the weight was 1,600lb (726kg) (300lb (136kg) over) and that the small engine lacked the required power. There was even objection to the fact that the manufacturer had used the more powerful Continental engine for the job instead of the Austin. Another complaint came from Col R. R. Robins that the Bantam was too high and underpowered. There was further criticism from the military that the ¼-ton 4×4 had a number of faults (to be expected surely?) and demanded too much maintenance. Then again, the differential and both axles 'went bad' after three months' testing.

The carping was limited, for Col Oseth called it a sensation. Bearing in mind that the Bantam was rushed together by hand, he made little of 'some minor grief' when the tail lights fell off owing to vibration. As Bantam had met the forty-nine-day limit for the initial model, it had the advantage of being able to put further prototypes in the field first, reaping goodwill and welcome recognition.

At this stage Bantam was by no means out of the story, but it is time to focus on Willys. The chairman of Willys-Overland was then Ward M. Canaday, whose interest in light reconnaissance vehicles for the army had been active from early 1939. The outbreak of war in Europe on 3 September of that year increased Canaday's interest since American involvement was very much on the cards. He had already on occasions talked with Col E. J. W. Proffitt of Ordnance about adapting the Willys car as a combat vehicle and provisional drawings were in existence. So now he contacted Col (later Brig Gen) H. J. Lawes, the commandant of the test centre at Camp Holabird, who suggested that Willys should build and submit a prototype. The ideas and the finance had to come from Willys.

After further consultation with Washington, Willys-Overland was able to clarify its plans and specifications for a light reconnaissance-type car which would suit various army needs. During the autumn of 1939 Willys discovered that Bantam was also trying to interest the army in similar fashion and had made a start, though neither company at that stage could have known the magnitude of what it was attempting. Afterwards Canaday said:

> It was our understanding, however, that the model they [Bantam] were developing was conceived to be primarily a substitute for the motorcycle with sidecar . . . to provide the infantry and cavalry with a protected messenger service of light and speedy general qualifications and three-man load capacity. This we looked upon as a conception very different from our own idea of a sturdy, powerful reconnaissance car.

In 1939 Willys was busy developing the lightweight 'Americar' and its engine for production in 1940. During this period the chief engineer 'Barney' Roos had been concentrating on the engine to improve power and fuel consumption without increasing either cubic capacity or weight. Without knowing it, Roos was providing the sort of engine that the army would require.

Roos, a former president of the Society of Automobile Engineers, thought (and Canaday agreed) that the emphasis should be on strength and power rather than all-up weight. He felt that it was impossible to build such a car to a weight limitation of 1,300lb (590kg) and to carry reliably a pay-load of 600lb (272kg). As the Willys approach was new, Col Lawes agreed, adding only that the weight should be kept as low as possible.

Willys-Overland built two prototypes, both of them with two- and four-wheel drive available, but one with four-wheel steering. Each had the Willys engine, because the engineering staff, from Roos down knew that it had both the power and the endurance. Furthermore, the engine's production line was available for immediate use. Ward

Canaday found in co-operation with the Army Quartermaster Corps that some of the military requirements were open to liberal interpretation. So strength and reliability remained more important than weight. The first Willys was put to the test at the Camp Holabird centre in Baltimore on 13 November 1940.

The Willys test driver, Donald Kenower, described what happened after the initial 5,000-mile (8,000-km) road run. The cross-country section had been laid out in a field to simulate rough terrain, including hills, ditches, rough sections, and so on. The Willys had light springing and army drivers were able to take the course – according to Kenower – twice as fast as in any other similar vehicle, the speed being determined by the crew's ability to 'stay *in* the job'. As is common on such occasions, there were problems. In Willys' case it was a faulty air-cleaner mounting. Heavy rains had made much of the field into a mud lake and enough of the mud had penetrated the engine via the air inlet to cause damage. To army engineers this was only straight cause and effect, so Willys quickly took an engine out of a passenger car and carried on.

By this stage in the story the military brass were in no doubt that they needed a ¼-ton 4×4 reconnaissance car in quantity, with the result that Henry Ford, king of mass production, was considered. Prominent figures like Col Lawes reputedly had doubts about Bantam's production capability for the very large numbers that would have to be ordered and delivered, and therefore invited Ford to take part. By 1940, however, Ford had moved away from producing small cars like the Model T and was not keen to join in.

The first seventy Bantam cars had been tested, resulting in the suggestion that the army should buy a further 1,500 for more widespread tests. It was at this stage that Ford agreed to co-operate and compete. Lt Col Henry S. Aurand was in charge of authorising purchase of the 4×4 and he suggested that orders might be placed for 1,500 each from Bantam, Willys and Ford. This proposal was agreed to, but with the proviso that both the Willys and Ford cars met the requirements already embodied in the Bantam. Ford agreed in December, following the contract placed with Bantam for a further 1,500, and prototypes were submitted. Known as the 'Pygmy', the Ford GP (General Purpose) had a tractor engine as this was the most suitable unit that Ford had in production. This, like the Continental engine in the Bantam, had 25 per cent less power than the Willys. Only the Willys had its own engine and furthermore it had the right performance characteristics. The military judges placed considerable importance on this engine, but it was 75lb (34kg) overweight. The main factor against Bantam was the doubt over production capacity, while for Ford their enormous production potential was an asset.

11

All three contenders were well over the original weight limit of 1,300lb (590kg), but the army in its final specification lifted this to 2,160lb (980kg). The Willys car weighed 2,423lb (1,100kg) and the company was told that the limit of 2,160lb (980kg) was final. Fortunately for Willys-Overland the Under-Secretary of War, Judge Patterson, intervened. On being told that there had been an understanding on weight flexibility between Col Lawes and the company, he approved an order for 1,500. Thus 4,500 were ordered, shared equally between the three companies.

At Willys, Ward Canaday commented that in spite of this success, orders in future would depend upon the weight being reduced to 2,160lb (980kg). On a power rating the Willys engine developed 60bhp, Bantam 40 and Ford 46, so Willys had the difficulty – in addition to engine weight – of needing a structure that would take around 50 per cent more power than its rivals. Barney Roos had to decide whether to redesign around the same engine or go into the market place for a different motor as Bantam had done with its Continental. He later pointed out that he knew from the military reports that the officers concerned liked the power and the performance it provided, and also the ride. He felt that if Willys were to buy in an engine, then existing advantages could be lost. In plain terms it would be pegging level with Bantam. The final decision – to stand by the Willys engine – must be among the most significant in the history of automobiles.

Roos and his colleagues were then faced with the task of taking off 263lb (approaching 2½cwt (119kg)) from an already spartan vehicle – seemingly a virtual impossibility. As an engineer, however, Roos understood every aspect of the task. Bit by bit he reduced the weight, often from places which the average engineer would have considered impossible or would not even have considered at all. He used higher-grade steel of less weight but the same strength. It reached a point where not only the weight of paint was important but even that of dust. He achieved the required weight with 7oz (200g) to spare.

The tributes to this feat flowed in. *Motor Industry* wrote in glowing terms about the vindication of Roos' lone voice which had been advocating the light automobile for years. A senior military spokesman said '. . . to retain the Willys engine . . . Roos met the weight by other changes, including weighing the paint. It was so closely within limit when it weighed in that if a little dust and dirt got on it that was enough to put it over the line'. He went on to say that the army wanted the Willys engine as it was and that 'Roos really "went to town" on reducing weight without interfering with the motor'. Among other tributes was that of Col Lawes, who described Roos as one of the most outstanding and capable motor engineers in the entire country.

First of the active line. The American Bantam model 40 BRC – 1940 *Bantam Reconnaissance Car* – equipped by the British Army for work in the desert. Note the Bren gun and 'skis' underneath to protect the transmission. This was the first ¼-ton 4×4 to arrive in Britain from the USA and to appear in the Western desert (*Imperial War Museum*)

Roots in the Mud

The conception of the Jeep dates back to the trenches and the muddy battlefields of World War I which were a personal hell for the infantry and played havoc with supply routes to the Front. The chief-of-staff of one general, their car struggling through the mud, was prompted to cry: 'Good God, did we really send men to fight in that?' History confirms that 8 million men lost their lives. The military planners thereafter sought to find a versatile alternative to the motorcycle-with-side car. The more far-seeing officers of the interwar period watched the development of all new military vehicles with gun-towing, cross-country supply-carrying and reconnaissance work in mind. Several military-units' engineers tried to build such a vehicle almost as a hobby interest.

The tempo of military activity in the USA speeded up when World War II broke out. US procedures for obtaining new equipment were explained later by Maj Gen C. L. Scott, when he was commander of the Armored Replacement base at Fort Knox, Kentucky. He said that the usual method was to set up the requirements as 'military character-istics'. In these were included the speed, height, armour, cross-country ability, number of crew, armament and necessary fighting qualities. He frequently sat on boards to establish equipment characteristics for both the cavalry and armoured wings, including those for the ¼-ton truck. He also pointed out that, in effect, there were many at the 'drawing board' who remained without credit for their contribution. Late in 1943 Gen Scott added some more information. He said that for years the cavalry had wanted a vehicle with the rough-terrain capability of a horse for the purposes of reconnaissance, carrying men, weapons and ammunition, and for communication. At the same time it had to be reasonably quiet and inconspicuous. Years before the production of such a vehicle many of its requisite characteristics had already been developed such as low profile and four-wheel drive, partly through trial and error.

Gen Scott added that when the cavalry had decided on their requirements, other branches such as the Ordnance and Quartermaster (Motor Transport) departments − and civilian automobile engineers − should endeavour to produce to the specification.

Brig Gen J. E. Barzynsky, CO of the Chicago Quartermaster Depot, wrote in 1941 that it was not surprising that many people had claimed credit for the Jeep's development. As such claims included false ones which might get absorbed incorrectly into Jeep history he directed Lt E. P. Hogan to research the subject for the records. Late in 1941 *The Quartermaster Review* carried an article by Hogan − by then a major − entitled 'The Story of the Quarter-ton, the Army's Smallest Car, Known as the Jeep'. It should be mentioned that in his opening sentence he had in mind mass-produced models like the famous Model T Ford − and was not in ignorance of the contributions of Daimler and Benz − when he referred to automobiles for the world!

He wrote that, in spite of the fact that America had given the world the original automobile, the small commercial car was not an American development. The *small* commercial car was designed in Europe to fill a need in thickly populated, comparatively small ground areas and because of the high cost of 'petrol'. In the USA where distances were greater and gasoline cheaper, there was not the same requirement for a small car. However, it was mainly from the small commercial car that the small military vehicle was developed.

Maj Hogan went on to write that, while there was no significant expansion in the US Army, the constantly increasing threat of war in Europe gave rise to a variety of suggestions for future military devel-opment. For at least ten years before the final advent of the Jeep the need was felt for a vehicle to replace the motorcycle-with-side car.

There is one reference after another to show that the experience of

World War I influenced the officers who served in it. Col William B. Johnson, supervising production of specifications at Holabird Quarter-master Depot in Baltimore, said that the development of the Jeep was 100 per cent due to the *need* for it experienced by army officers in World War I. Maj Gen R. M. Danford, who was Chief of Field Artillery, said that 'the Jeep is the outgrowth of military characteristics evolved by many army men throughout a long period of years'. This comment was confirmed by Maj Gen E. B. Gregory, the Quarter-master General, stressing the need for four-wheel drive. Confirmation also came from Brig Gen F. L. Parks, Assistant Commander of the 69th Infantry Division: 'Many army officers of my acquaintance have discussed with me such a vehicle since World War I. I do not know any one individual from whom the idea sprung. The need was apparent to many who worked with motor transportation.'

Further comment came from Brig Gen E. W. Fales, then commanding the Infantry Replacement Centre in Florida. He concurred, but added that the infantry requested a vehicle in which all the essential characteristics were united for the first time in a way practical for both production and operation. In many cases, he said, various combinations had been tried but found to be useless.

Fundamentally, the Jeep was a vehicle to take over from the horse, especially for the infantry. Officers who had seen active service in World War I had endured the suffering not just of themselves and their men but also of their horses. Apart from those animals which died from wounds, many died simply from starvation for lack of fodder in battle. Motor transport became increasingly reliable and versatile, and the development of fast, light tanks was changing the pattern of warfare in which the horse had no place.

The Jeep covered these needs and, significantly, so many more besides. It did more than any other military vehicle to increase mobility and change the face of army tactics.

Forerunners of the Jeep

If the Jeep was a product of technical evolution allied to military needs, there were progenitors. One group, for example, goes back to 1921 and was described by Col C. C. Terry of Ordnance in a paper he wrote in 1944 called 'Test and Development of Light Cross-country Vehicles at Aberdeen Proving Grounds, Maryland'. In this he recorded that some fifteen light vehicles were tested in 1921 for their cross-country ability. The design purposes of these varied, some were for light transport, others for reconnaissance, and others again for all-round ability. The primary intention was to improve on the motor-cycle, with or without sidecar, used in World War I.

A 'motor-cart' developed in 1923 can also be included among those vehicles which led up to the Jeep. This unique vehicle came from Fort Benning, Georgia, and was powered by a motorcycle engine. As with a motor-mower the operator walked behind it. Measuring 8ft 6in (2.5m) long, it was of aluminimum and waterproof. It could therefore carry a fair-sized load on land or water, but one snag was that it had no propeller. Once the wheels were out of their depth the operator had to guide it by swimming, pushing or poling, and was able to climb aboard to rest only in favourable conditions.

The chief automotive engineer of the Ordnance Technical Division, W. F. Beasley, confirmed that the motor-cart was a full army-sponsored venture, undertaken on the recommendation of an Ordnance Board, which wanted to develop a cross-country reconnaissance vehicle capable of travelling through water. He has put on record that Col Terry (at that time a captain) drew up the report of this Ordnance Board; it also contained a reference to a ¼-ton tractor that had been under consideration in 1919–20.

At that time the Quartermaster Corps and Ordnance wanted a reconnaissance car which could carry supplies, including ammunition. Even at this early stage a low profile was to be an aspect of the design. Of the fifteen light vehicles tested in 1921 one by-no-means-new Dodge was modified to be front runner in any claims to be the first half-track. The Model T Ford was also adapted to have belt tracks, and Col Terry claims that this was some five years before the famous crossing of the Sahara Desert by Citroën using rubber half-tracks. In this connection the 'Who was first?' aspect is of no account, but what is more important was the development work going on continuously, development which finally produced the Jeep.

Some of the tracked vehicles which continued to be tested at Aberdeen, Maryland, were thought to be of designs masterminded by Maj W. A. Capron of Ordnance. Having plain aluminium bodies they were nicknamed 'Capron's Silver Fish'. However, this proved to be an exercise in finding out just how many mistakes or miscalculations could be made.

Progress continued, but credit for later development goes to Gen L. H. Campbell Jr (Chief of Ordnance in 1942 but at that time a major at Aberdeen proving ground). Because of unease about the tested half-tracks Campbell decided that a car, stripped of inessentials and with very low gearing, would be the answer for cross-country work. A Model T was chosen for the test. This was stripped down to the chassis, cutting the weight down to no more than 1,200lb (544kg). Performance was improved, but the high-pressure tyres – with a width of only 3–3½in (76–89mm) – lost adhesion on difficult terrain. The next step was to modify the wheels to take wider aircraft tyres.

This is believed to be the progenitor of the 'balloon tyre'.

W. F. Beasley made this reasonable claim and went on to say that it made a great difference. The Model T was then fitted with two bucket seats and a platform body, with canvas as protection from the wind. The result was the lightest vehicle to date . . . 'and it embodied the basic idea of the present-day standardized Jeep'.

Col Terry, writing about it, said in effect that the performance put paid to belt-tracked light vehicles for, in spite of snags, its ability on soft-going was far superior. The vehicle prompted concentration on the lightweight, wheeled car which eventually resulted in the Jeep. Meantime, this was the end of any combination that included water-crossing ability when out of its depth.

According to Beasley the Services made so many extra demands, including even cushion seating, that the weight went up to that of an ordinary car, ruining the basic idea.

Almost certainly the most significant forerunner of the true Jeep was the ½-ton Ford developed by Marmon-Herrington of Indianapolis. This began with a conversion of the Ford 1½-ton truck. In the early 1930s farsighted people in Europe and America could see the need for more modern military equipment in the event of a second world war. For example, in England Mitchell foresaw the equipment which enabled the Battle of Britain to be won, while in the Jeep story Arthur W. Herrington, a World War I colonel and President of Marmon-Herrington, realised the necessity of a military vehicle.

Herrington's company had become famous for multi-wheel drive, heavy-duty vehicles of up to 25-ton capacity. He saw that as well as the heavy military carriers (including gun carriers) already being built there was a need for something lighter and more mobile, and with the best possible cross-country ability. This was in 1934, but it was later, in an atmosphere of greater urgency, that Marmon-Herrington converted a 1½-ton Ford to all-wheel drive. This was much heavier than the light reconnaissance car that the military had in mind but the characteristics were such that army thinking developed further: for example, Herrington had shown that it was possible to convert a vehicle already in volume production.

Two years earlier, on a visit to Europe in 1936, Herrington had interested the Belgian government in the 1½-ton conversion, but after much deliberation the Belgians, too, wanted something lighter. After this the company started on plans for converting the Ford ½-ton truck, a vehicle originally intended for light deliveries. Late in 1936, after tough testing, it was sent to Belgium. In the following June the US War Department made its first purchase of five, designated LD-1. Further orders followed during a period of eighteen months, the vehicle being nicknamed the 'Darling'.

Extensive testing began early in 1938, after which the testing report added:

To those who have been thinking of infantry weapons-and-ammunition carriers as track-laying vehicles, these tests furnish food for thought. The results certainly merit a reconsideration of our ideas on this subject. In spite of any prejudices to the contrary, it must be noted that throughout the test, the ½-ton, 4×4 truck crossed obstacles where the other vehicles failed. Furthermore, in addition to its regular load, it towed the anti-tank guns across obstacles that could not be crossed by the tractors without a load. As a matter of interest, it may be added that a mule was unable to pull the 81mm mortar cart with a 500lb [227kg] pay-load up slopes that were easily climbed by the truck.

The use of a truck as a weapons-and-ammunition carrier reduces to a minimum the undesirable features common to all tractors, such as high initial cost, short mechanical life, expensive maintenance and operation, mechanical unreliability, and necessity for specially trained drivers and mechanics.

In view of the outstanding performance of the ½-ton, 4×4 truck, this vehicle is believed to be the best of its type available at present. Certainly it has demonstrated that it can perform suitably the following functions for infantry units: ammunition carrier, weapons carrier, communication equipment carrier, and prime mover for the 37mm anti-tank gun.

As a result of this report an order was made in early 1939 by the War Department for sixty-four of these ½-ton, versatile vehicles. Drive through all four wheels was clearly the deciding factor. The number was decided after an appraisal of the military needs at that time. On entering service the 'Darling' became 'Our Darling' among the troops using it. This vehicle was a true ancestor of the Jeep, with its low profile, load-carrying capacity, and what was then the creditable speed of 35mph (56kph).

It has been mentioned that both military and civilian engineers between the wars were working on what proved to be the Jeep theme, sometimes without any financial backing, and often through the enthusiasm of those with suitable workshops and access to 'bits and pieces' (mainly the army). In the middle thirties a Capt Robert G. Howie visited motor manufacturers in Detroit and elsewhere, without it being realised that he was doing this while on leave and at his own expense. Among students of automotive history Howie is famous, but first the story of his activities which also led to the development of the Jeep.

Howie at that time was interested in midget racing cars and knowledgeable about small engines and the transmissions, axles, wheels, and so on. His name is best remembered for the Howie-Wiley machine-gun carrier. Gen L. McD. Silvester, commanding the US

Seventh Armored Division, put on record his opinion that Howie's ideas — which resulted in the development of the carrier — led in turn to the later development of the Jeep.

The carrier was finally the product of Howie's work in conjunction with Master Sgt Melvin C. Wiley at the Fort Benning Infantry School. Like the later Jeep this was a ¼-ton vehicle, but with the engine at the back and the drive at the front. The principle, which applies in the many front-wheel-drive cars of today, was that you could pull more than you could push. At the back the engine was over the type of axle normally used at the front. In development four-wheel-drive was adopted, after advice and help from the Timken-Detroit Axle Company. Work did not begin in real earnest until the beginning of 1937. Nearly all the parts were either stock items for vehicles already in production or were machined by Wiley. Junk piles were scoured for anything useful. Many parts were Austin, including the 4-cylinder water-cooled engine.

Tests by the Infantry Board resulted in praise generally. On the other side of the coin, however, cross-country ability was limited because of the small wheels, despite their fat tyres. There were no springs. In effect, it was a platform on which a crew of two could lie prone, thus offering a minimum silhouette.

The claim that this little buggy was the grandfather of the Jeep carries more credence in the light of the following events. In March 1940 Barney Roos was invited to a demonstration where he at once visualised a low-silhouette, ultra-mobile vehicle built for military purposes but based on the Willys light car. He reported his views at staff level.

At about this time a military committee with Lt Col W. F. Lee of the Chief of Infantry's Office was working along similar lines. Col Howie told how he was sent to American Bantam accompanied by a civilian engineer called Brown (of the War Department).

> Brown left after some seven or eight days, and I stayed on another week or ten days to work out details of body design, power plant, clearance, cross-country characteristics, wheel and tyre size, etc. I turned over all my blueprints, specifications, etc, to the Bantam Company.

A member of the Technical Board who was present wrote:

> Each member of the committee got in one of their [Bantam's] cars and took it out on a race track where we played follow-the-leader and did all kinds of stunts inside the track enclosure. Then we took all the cars out and tried them across country for half a day. Then the army engineers . . . and I, at the direction of the committee, got together to draw up the military characteristics of the vehicle we felt the army required.

First, we designated four-wheel drive; second, the wheelbase; third, the width and height; fourth, crew of three men; fifth, armament, a 0.30-cal machine gun mounted on a pedestal; sixth, engine power; seventh, performance maximum; eighth, cooling to permit a low speed of three miles [5kph] per hour; ninth, cross-country performance and grade-climbing ability; tenth, standard multi-wheel-drive cargo vehicle; eleventh, ground clearance of not less than 6¼in [158mm] at the axle centre.

At that stage it was thought that Bantam had adequate production facilities. The chief of infantry then collated all this information and finally the quartermaster general sent out the message to the unprecedented number of 135 companies.

The Bantam saga would not be complete without reference to Harold Crist. He was plant manager at Bantam and put the car through its paces for the committee. He had been with Stutz in Indianapolis for eighteen years where he had built racing cars and where he proved to be a driver of the highest class. Brown, the civilian engineer, worked with Crist on the general specifications. The most significant factor was that they agreed that the (first Jeep) proposed vehicle would have to be new rather than designed round the Bantam.

When the invitations to tender were put out to the 135 companies – with only Bantam at first taking up the challenge – the specifications owed much to Harold Crist.

2
SELECTION OF THE WINNER

The contest for the coveted prize of what was to be known later as the Jeep reached its final phase after the army purchase of 1,500 models each from Bantam, Willys and Ford. Everything was arranged for the final testing to be run by the Army Quartermaster Corps. Also represented were the cavalry, infantry, field artillery, armoured corps and the engineers. Here is the US Army tentative specification (LP-997A):

1 A level road maximum speed of not less than fifty-five (55) miles per hour [88kph] at an engine speed that does not exceed the peak horsepower speed.

2 A level road minimum speed of not more than three (3) miles per hour [5kph].

3 An ability to ford (hard-bottom) water crossings of at least eighteen (18) inches [460mm] of water depth at a speed of at least three (3) miles per hour [5kph] without effect from the water.

4 Tire chains are required for use on driving wheel tires, and frequently will be used when traversing hazardous terrain. The truck construction shall permit the satisfactory installation and use of the tire chains.

5 The weight of the truck fully equipped (including lubricants and water), but less fuel, tire chains and payload, shall not exceed twenty-one hundred (2,100) pounds [950kg] for two (2) wheel steer trucks, and twenty-one hundred and seventy-five (2,175) pounds [987kg] for four (4) wheel steer trucks, and every effort, consistent with best recognized engineering practices, shall be made to minimize the weight.

6 The payload allowance shall be eight hundred (800) pounds [363kg] for operating personnel (including the driver) and military equipped wheels.

7 The angle of approach shall be at least forty-five (45) degrees; angle of departure at least thirty-five (35) degrees, with the truck fully equipped, loaded and in a level position.

This was a formidable specification indeed. For readers who may not grasp the last condition, it means that the sudden change from level ground to 45° had to be achieved without the lower front of the car touching the slope. Coming off such a slope to level ground the brakes would be on in all probability and weight transfer to the front is allowed for in the lesser angle of 35°.

The three competitors racing to satisfy the military demand for the

The Willys Quad of 1940: a one-piece screen, no central support for the canvas top. The front grille was the most distinguishing feature

¼-ton 4×4 made the qualifying weight, and the battle between 4,500 cars was joined in test centres, proving grounds and in everyday usage right across the country. Countless evaluators sought out faults and failures from the most serious to the comparatively trivial. Throughout the age of the automobile, prototype models have had their share of problems to be sorted out; if we think back to all the circumstances of the birth of these three models, and the time element involved (bearing in mind that World War II was already well under way in Europe with allied forces badly needing supplies of such a vehicle), the number of problems was remarkably small.

It is history that Willys-Overland won, but the manner in which it did so is authoritatively recorded in the comments of many adjudicators. All the following comments made at the time or in retrospect are from people like Maj C. A. Stein of the Field Artillery School in North Carolina; Maj J. W. Knott (Artillery); Maj J. C. Dotson (instructor); and the colonels most closely related to the project.

The Ford often had locked transmission trouble; due to the arrangement of the shift lever, the fork would move out. Vapor locks occurred in the gas line where it was close to the exhaust or other heated parts of the engine . . . underpowered engine . . . mud-sucker generator . . . and the tie-rod was in front of the axle, always being bent against stumps.

Another comment was about breakdowns 'because of the weight over the rear axle', and 'because it was too low'. Other criticisms included lack of power and the timing requiring a lot of tuning.

The artillery reported that the Bantam had many faults. A steering jerk would cause it to dive to the left; the shock absorbers were very poor and the too-light battery support required frequent welding. The Bantam passenger-car type of transmission was too light for the task. The gears soon wore out, although later they were strengthened. The transmission was positioned too low, for the army found the need for sleds under it in some cross-country circumstances. Another transmission fault was that the synchromesh was too weak.

There was a credit side, however. The engine was thought better than Ford's. The Ford had a generator which had mud sucked into it by the fan. The early Ford had the V-unit tractor engine without synchromesh, thus involving double declutching, and it needed weekly tuning. One summary of the Ford and Bantam engines was that the Ford was designed for governor-controlled speed, and there was bearing trouble; the radiator on the Bantam caused overheating, for example in sandy going. The Bantam was beaten on power and performance by the Ford.

Col R. R. Robins said that there was a great deal of difference between the three cars, but again he was impressed with the power-to-weight ratio of the Willys and the durability of its engine. Col Oseth, an important adjudicator, said afterwards that all three models were satisfactory, but all the troops had a preference for the Willys because of its power. It was the difference between 45 and 60bhp. In *Hail to the Jeep!* by A. W. Wade in 1946 the author pointed out rightly that although the Willys engine was, so to speak, on every lip, its popularity was not the sole factor in the ultimate decision. This was also influenced by the car's ruggedness while yet keeping within weight specifications.

In an article called 'The Jeep in Action' in *Army Ordnance* in the autumn of 1944 Maj E. P. Hogan made a summary of the factors influencing the decision in favour of Willys:

From the original pilot models submitted by Bantam, Ford Motor Company, and Willys-Overland Motors Inc, which were tested again and again on one of the stiffest courses in the country at the old Holabird Quartermaster Depot in Baltimore, and from the 1,500 built by each of

Willys started with the Quad on the left. Next is the famous MB, standard from its inception for the remainder of hostilities. Then came the single windshield M38 in 1950 and the more curvaceous M38A1 in 1951. Here is the best-known quartet

these manufacturers in 1941, the Willys model was finally chosen by Army engineers as coming the closest to meeting Army requirements. The Willys bid was lower and the Willys engine had greater power. However, the decision to standardize on the Willys model was reached only after gruelling tests on manoeuvers and in Army camps from one end of America to the other.

Willys's advantages resulted in an initial order for 16,000 − later increased to 18,600.

The sad elimination of Bantam from the contest was due essentially to its lack of production facilities to cope with the number of cars involved. One of the arbiters, Col Van Deusen, said that further investigation was made about production facilities and concluded: 'They just could produce an assembly, all of which they bought. They used the Spicer axle and their only production was the bodywork.'

The US Army planners deserve credit for recognising the risk of sabotage or bombing and insisted on two suppliers. It was an

interesting situation to have two major manufacturers producing the same vehicle. Remember that at this time the USA was not at war and the automotive firms were in direct competition.

It was in this situation that Quartermaster General E. B. Gregory heard that Edsel Ford was in Washington DC. As Gregory, in the company of Brig Gen (now) H. J. Lawes and Col Van Deusen, went to find Ford it happened that they met by chance in the Railroad Retirement Board HQ. Gen Gregory said that the army wanted to standardise on the approved (Willys) job. He pointed out that, with the need of two sources of supply, Edsel Ford and his company could be doing the army and the country an immeasurable service by manufacturing the Willys design with the Willys engine and all other parts interchangeable. In the circumstances Edsel Ford's reply, without hesitation, was remarkable: 'Gentlemen, the answer is yes.'

As a result Willys made available to Ford — free — all the specifications and patents for the ¼-ton 4×4 truck.

Why Jeep?

Tracking down the origin of a name which has become a household word is not as easy as it seems. There is also the factor that when a trade name is used as a generic name — such as Hoover for a vacuum cleaner or Thermos for a vacuum flask — further complications arise. So let it be understood that today Jeep is registered in the name of American Motors Corporation. The 'J' is therefore always a capital letter; one cannot go by jeep but perhaps by a Jeep-type vehicle, which can only mean a 4×4 of similar size — but even this may insult a JEEP!

During the development days there were many nicknames. A typical one was 'Blitz Buggy' and another was 'Puddle Jumper'. Certainly, no one would seriously be expected to call this versatile vehicle the 'quarter-ton four-by-four' every time. 'Jeep' first came into use for the early Willys and the story of how it came about is well authenticated. So this tends to rule out the popular explanation that the (*General Purpose*) Ford GP (*Gee Pee*) accounted for the name. Also during tests, GP changed to GCA.

The one man behind the name seems to be Irving 'Red' Hausmann, Willys-Overland test driver at Toledo, Ohio. This name was even then not original, as will be seen, but Hausmann used it with constant deliberateness. The choice proved to be perfect, for it was taken up officially by Willys-Overland and it 'clicked' everywhere with everyone.

Hausmann's story is that he drove the first Willys prototype to Holabird with co-driver Don Kenower. Shortly afterwards the Ford competitor arrived, so some distinction had to be made. Hausmann took pride in 'his' vehicle and did not like confusion with other names like 'Bantam', 'Bug', 'Midget', 'Ford GP', 'Quad' or 'Peep'. He picked 'Jeep' from the competition, so to speak, getting approval from troops who were chewing over various names. Jeep came out on top, and thereafter Hausmann used the name constantly and it soon became universal to identify the Willys. When he returned to Toledo, his department fell into line.

There is confirmation of this story by Barney Roos, the engineering expert behind the design and development of the Jeep, and also by Donald S. Stone who was head of the research department. It seems established that 'Jeep' was used only in connection with the Willys. Further support for this came from Col Duell who said that the name was not used for the early Bantam model. All this was in 1940 during the test period when all the tight schedules had to be met. No newspaper at that time used the name other than for the Willys.

The final public recognition of the name Jeep came probably in February 1941, when Red Hausmann gave a demonstration run to Katherine Hillyer of the Washington *Daily News*. Hausmann put the Willys through its paces with test-driver's aplomb and at the end an outsider asked the name. Red answered, 'It's a Jeep.' Inevitably the

Testing the Ford GP Pygmy at Holabird in late 1940. This had the Ferguson 'Dearborn' tractor engine and the Ford Model A gearbox (*Imperial War Museum*)

journalist used this name in her copy and the photograph had the name in its caption. The feature appeared on 19 February 1941.

Earlier on the same day Hausmann had driven the car up – and down – the steps of the Capitol building in Washington DC closely covered by the national press. From that point the name, repeated in newspapers and other journals, was so established that even those military objectors to such informality changed their minds and Jeep became the official name. For example, when a military author (Maj E. P. Hogan) wrote a history of the Jeep development in 1941 he was at first refused permission to include the word in his sub-title, but by the time he had finished his research and compilation he had approval to do so.

The public at large accepted Jeep without considering the word's origin, and popular songs of the day included it, for example, 'Six Jerks in a Jeep', 'Four Jills in a Jeep' and 'Little Bo Peep has lost her Jeep'.

At that time one of the animals in the famous cartoon series *Popeye* was Eugene the Jeep, who appeared from 1937. Like Popeye, he was a creation of the late E. C. Segar (King Features Syndicate Inc). Segar

Elan! A favourite Jeep picture of two GIs having fun with a Ford GP

described the Jeep as an invisible fourth-dimensional creature of Africa who lived on orchids. He could become three-dimensional and visible, however, and was able to foresee the future. Hausmann may well have had this magical creature in mind when he produced the name. The mechanical Jeep, after all, could do almost anything.

Research into the origin of the name Jeep revealed that this was far from being the first vehicle of that name. In 1936 the Halliburton Oil Well Cementing Co used the name Jeep for a geological vehicle which used electricity for recording survey work. As Eugene the Jeep was given an electric tail the source of the name must be the same. There were problems over copyright between King Features and Halliburton, but gradually Halliburton dropped the name Jeep. However, in 1938 the Halliburton company president used an animal from Honduras with an appearance similar to the cartoon Jeep at an international exhibition but, even so, the name was no longer used commercially.

One claim to be the first using the Jeep name was made by W. C. MacFarlane, President of the Minneapolis-Moline Power Implement

The late E. C. Segar originated the *Popeye* cartoons. They marketed spinach without doubt but, it seems, also spawned Jeeps. This is the miraculous Eugene the Jeep, dating back to 1936. It could do anything — and so could the ¼-ton 4×4 that was to follow (© *1937 King Features Syndicate, Inc*)

Co, whose tractor was adapted for military purposes, and which was called Jeep by the sergeant driver James T. O'Brien. It was demonstrated before the adjutant general in 1937, but the first printed use of the name did not appear until the autumn of 1940 in the St Paul *Pioneer Press*. For about a year from that time the name was used for this heavy vehicle, but by then it was also being used for the Jeep as we know it.

Another claim to the name was made for an autogiro designed for military purposes. Col H. F. Gregory was the instigator of the name in this instance. A Col G. F. Johnston claimed that the name was given to the Y-17 aircraft tested in 1937–8, but was dropped because the name of the little magical creature Eugene the Jeep was inappropriate to an aircraft of such large size. Col Johnston also said that a toy Jeep had been given to Col Gregory because of the autogiro, and had this machine gone into squadron service then Jeep would have been the badge, as permission had been given by the cartoonist and his syndicators. However, the giro was overtaken by other alternatives and the Jeep name faded with it.

All this by no means completes the argument, which rages indefinitely among etymologists. For another example, Maj E. P. Hogan talked about it with army transport officers in the days of the Quartermaster Motor Transport Service and informed them that it was an old army workshop term for any new vehicle received for test. The armoured branch also used it, but not in relation to the ¼-ton scout car. In the latter case the name stuck as a result of general public use.

Furthermore, there is the Peep-Jeep controversy. As late as December 1943, Col Claude A. Black wrote on the subject from Fort Knox. He said that in the army the ¼-ton vehicle was called a Peep. The true Jeep in army parlance was the ½-ton counterpart. He admitted, however, that the public had won and the smaller vehicle was known as Jeep.

Lexicographers have researched the origin of the word Jeep. For example, did it pre-date both the *Popeye* cartoon creature and the ¼-ton truck? Soon after the war the publishers of *Webster's International Dictionary* favoured the GP (General Purpose) influenced by the name of the cartoon character. In research *Encyclopaedia Britannica* quoted an article in December 1943 by the distinguished authority H. L. Mencken (author of *The American Language*). Mencken in his turn raised the matters of GP and Segar's cartoons, but then said that his inclination was in line with that of John B. Opdycke — another well-known writer on language usage. Opdycke's definition was given in full:

Jeep: Name of the acrobatic army reconnaissance car, appropriately rhyming with leap; contraction of GP, general purpose, the design originally having a number and being ordered in War Department correspondence as GPO, No. –: orders came in so thick and fast that they were designated GP, and, perhaps under the influence of a popular moving picture comic strip, employees came to reduce the letters to Jeep. In World War I a new recruit was called a cookie, now an almost archaic word in this sense, for today he is called a jeep, which is definitely derived from the comic strip.

However, Mencken still asked: 'JEEP. Can anyone supply the true etymology and history of *jeep?*'

There are and have been people called Jeep including one in Gibbon's *Decline and Fall* . . . (Rugby enthusiasts in England may also think that their former international Richard Jeeps was aptly named, for the 's' could indicate more than one of him on the field!) There are also US servicemen with the name Jeep, which may be a slight embarrassment to them. Take your choice, but the ¼-ton 4×4 is called a JEEP.

The Famous MB

As soon as Willys-Overland had been awarded the order for 16,000 of its winning design, designated MA, it was time to make final appraisal and to decide what changes, if any, needed to be made for the standardised version. Inevitably changes were made, but it is significant that while some were made at the suggestion of the army and others by Willys itself, such was the spirit of everyone concerned with development, and indeed their genuine affection for the car, that the ultimate result was all that mattered. Changes from the pilot models can be listed:

1 An improved air cleaner for the induction to meet government specifications.

2 A bigger generator for the 6V system with a 40A max output. This was known as the standard QMC (Quartermaster Corps) unit used with a government standard regulator. Changes of this sort were basically for standardisation among military trucks – if necessary one could cannibalise.

3 The fuel tank had to be increased in capacity by half to 15 US gal (54 litres). This, not surprisingly, turned out to be a problem, finally solved by extending the tank outside the frame but still within the overall width of the bodyshell.

4 Army engineers settled for 5in (127mm) sealed beam headlamps with double filament bulb.

5 Instead of the battery as used in the Willys car of the day, standardisation called for the government 2-H unit used on so many other military vehicles and therefore interchangeable.

6 The handbrake was moved to a central position within reach of the front passenger.

7 Next came the remote control gear lever (shift). Preference was for the direct lever centrally mounted. One reason for this was the maintenance of standard practice as far as possible so that an army driver could change from one vehicle to another with minimum appraisal of the positions of the controls.

8 One of the telling points in favour of the Willys had been the position of the steering tie-rods, high above the front suspension, out of danger on rough ground. This feature was further enhanced.

9 Extra protection had to be made for the security of hydraulic brake hose both at front and rear.

10 Willys engineers improved support of the canvas top by suggesting two tubular hoops instead of the earlier single one. Head-room for the driver was increased without change in the all-important silhouette.

The traditional MB; this one belongs to the automobile artist Michael Turner *(Ron Easton)*

11 In earlier tests it was found that the spring shackles needed too much attention. So army engineers from Holabird devised seals for protection against muck and water. This increased the life of the shackles by three times and also reduced the need for lubrication by a factor of three.

12 The British Pioneer Corps was well known, to those old enough to remember, for having the hard labouring job of digging earthworks, and so on. In the USA the same term is used and government engineers wanted pioneer tools. This meant the provision on the left-hand side of the body for a shovel and an axe.

13 Lighting equipment was brought into line with the standardisation already existing on other military vehicles. Included were black-out driving lamps at the front and black-out tail and stop lights at the back.

14 An army request was for a power take-off. This had not been incorporated in earlier models but was later made a category of special equipment for the marine corps and the navy.

Production started but inevitably there were last-minute thoughts. The tyres were increased from 5.50 to 6.00. Heavier wheels were also adopted, with a split rim. This had the added advantage of permitting the car to continue for a long way when a tyre was flat. Provision was

The MB shown from the back. Note that the top has an extra support in the middle. The civilian number plate is an extra, which is usually taken off for display purposes. Other items are described in Chapter 6 (*Ron Easton*)

made for the famous jerricans to be located at the back as a fuel reserve. These were of 5 US gal (19 litres) capacity, which explains the slightly odd 4½ imperial gal (20 litres) capacity when used in the UK theatres of war. Also an extra black-out lamp was fitted low down on the left.

Provision also had to be made for a trailer rear light because a ¼-ton trailer was on the stocks for use with the Jeep. This took the form of a standard government socket. A more important and difficult task was radio suppression. One must remember that at that time car radio scarcely existed, unlike today when all cars have their high-tension circuit to the spark plugs suppressed. It was not only the 'sparks' of the Jeep but also of other nearby vehicles that had to be suppressed. As is now commonplace, this meant earthing the sources of interference, with the extra use of condensers as necessary. This was something new and the problem was sorted out in conjunction with the Signal Corps. So, after two months, vehicles were coming off the production line fully suppressed as standard.

The outcome was the famous MB model which was to continue,

The 'cockpit'. To the right of the orthodox gear lever is the lever for bringing in FWD, and to the right of that is the ratio change. Under a fixed cover just below the screen is an M1 carbine (*Ron Easton*)

built by Willys and Ford, to the end of World War II and beyond under the aegis of American Motors. The Humvee will take over (see Chapter 5). While the final models were going into production, however, the military version of the German 'people's car', the Volkswagen, was already in action. The latter had been among Hitler's confidence tricks, thousands of his countrymen innocently making advance payments not for a people's car at all but for an additional implement of war. Designed by the late Dr Ferdinand Porsche (who achieved fame for the extraordinary, quality fast cars known worldwide today), the use of an air-cooled, horizontally opposed 4-cylinder engine with its weight over the rear driving wheels provided – and still does in its civilian form – exceptional traction in difficult conditions. Dr Porsche, however, was more concerned with the design of a true people's car than with military transport. The teamwork which went into the Jeep put the two designs poles apart for military purposes.

When a captured Volkswagen (bearing the badge of Rommel's

The MB engine from the right. Note that the oil filter is as easy to get at as the large air filter. The distributor can be reached equally easily (*Ron Easton*)

Afrika Korps) was put to the test against the Jeep it was strictly a 'no contest'. The military VW was good for speeds up to 30mph (48kph) so, but could not cover rough going which the Jeep could take in its stride at 50mph (80kph).

In a letter to the *Scientific American* Maj J. H. Chamberlin of the Air Corps included the following comment:

Gruelling tests showed that the Jeep could fight as well as run and it could go places a motorcycle couldn't. Besides, a motorcycle dispatch rider is vulnerable; a single sniper can cut him down, letting vital orders fall into enemy hands. A Jeep, carrying armed men and machine guns, is a far tougher proposition. And, vital for combat strategy, the Jeep is a clawing, climbing hellion in reaching good places to shoot from.

In Mississippi I learned first-hand what it was like to ride in a Jeep across pine-studded acres at 50mph [80kph]. I learned also that much of its effectiveness depends on the driver's boldness and ability. It was like driving a Model T Ford across a ploughed field. I was riding a steel bronco, held loosely in my seat by a safety belt. Lt Summerour rocked easily beside

The left-hand side of the engine is also easy to reach for adjustments to the carburettor. Note the pipe from sump to carburettor, providing an oil mist to the combustion chambers (*Ron Easton*)

me as though cantering his horse in Central Park, apparently enjoying the ride.

He slowed down our Jeep and straddled a half-burnt log, front wheels tilted to the sky. I visualized a shattered crank case but was shown guide bars underneath for just such protection. Grabbing special handles on the body, we lifted the car and shoved it easily off the log.

Maj Chamberlin wrote of the admiration of army strategists for the low profile of only 3⅓ft (1.05m), making it even more difficult to align in an enemy's sights. Remembering Lt Summerour's drive, the major recalled driving under what seemed to be almost ground-touching branches with the need only to duck, at which point the leg and arm room were appreciated. Next came a ford with water 18in (460mm) deep; again there was no problem as the Jeep's electrics are placed high up. Finally came a 30° slope, much steeper than any incline on any public road. All these remarks were typical of the Services' reaction to the finished Jeep.

Of interest here are the steering, wheel drive and telescopic suspension dampers (*Ron Easton*)

In any vehicle the engine is the heart of the matter, and where the Jeep was concerned it was a mixture of careful earlier design and development, some luck in its timing, and the availability in quantity production. Without the special needs dictated by military consider-ations the engine was that of the Willys car up to the time of Pearl Harbor (1941). When pilot Jeeps had to be produced Ward Canaday and Barney Roos knew that they had something in this four-cylinder unit. It was strong, but at that time the power output was only 45bhp.

Roos joined Willys-Overland as chief engineer in 1938 after establishing his ability with Pierce Arrow (now treasured vintage cars), Locomobile and Studebaker. The Willys engine giving its 45bhp at 3,400rpm was already established, but Roos — while leaving the bore and stroke unchanged — up-rated the engine to 60bhp at 4,000rpm. During this further development Roos had to work on a tight budget, so this achievement was remarkable.

Roos' approach was to take an engine off the production line and run it at its optimum power speed of 3,400rpm. After 22min, rod bearings

It is curious that no one has taken up the Jeep idea to hinge a headlamp in the event of an engine breakdown in the dark (*Ron Easton*)

collapsed and the cylinders were well worn. The cooling system was then modified and the pistons were made of tin-plated aluminium. These were the significant changes, which resulted in an achievement of 50 hours' run at 3,600rpm. At this stage the valves gave up. Roos continued with his inspired empirical method until the engine would run at 4,000rpm for 100 hours without failure, which became the standard test.

The army required other modifications, including mountings to suit the Jeep, better performance on very steep slopes by induction and carburettor alterations and, because of likely operational conditions, special army air and oil filters. Further information about Roos the man appeared in *Modern Industry* in April 1943, which mentioned his love of locomotives.

He has never lost his first desire to be a designer of iron horses and he will climb into the cab at the slightest invitation. But at the moment he is busy designing more combat vehicles, modifications of the Jeep which will take it into the air, and make it suitable for radio and tractor work. He's spawning specialized Jeeps to link the name Jeep and Roos even closer.

Field officers up to the rank of general praised the Jeep in every possible way, but it was probably the thousands of other users at a lower level who proved them right.

WILLYS MB DATES OF PRODUCTION

1941	MB 100 001 – 108 598	
1942	MB 108 599 – 200 022	
1943	MB 200 023 – 293 232	
1944	MB 293 233 – 402 334	
1945	MB 402 335 – 459 851	

3
THE JEEP IN ACTION

Before the USA entered the war in December 1941, Jeeps were already being supplied to the United Kingdom, which at that time stood alone against the Nazi onslaught. There can scarcely be anyone in the British Army, and later many other forces, who did not become familiar with the Jeep at some stage; and most have their favourite Jeep stories to tell. As the war progressed there were few important statesmen and generals who had not visited battle areas or combat troops seated in a Jeep. Among these was Franklin Delano Roosevelt, US President.

A. W. Wade in his *Hail to the Jeep!* wrote that:

Of all the millions of pieces of military equipment that America, 'the arsenal of democracy', poured forth from her prodigious industries for use in World War II, no other implement of war became so famous. In winning the favor of United Nations (allied) troops everywhere, the Jeep became America's foremost goodwill ambassador in the war.

This, as the present author recalls, was if anything an understatement – certainly no exaggeration.

Some of Wade's anecdotes are of special interest, gathered as they were just after the end of the war. Many relate to the variety of uses to which the Jeep was put with success, from warding off enemy attacks using 0.50 calibre machine-guns to carrying seven men if necessary, as the extras rode side-saddle on the front bumpers. He wrote that from the time it first fought with the British in Burma and later at the victory of El Alamein, the Jeep advanced from triumph to triumph . . . until it became a legend the world over.

Among the anecdotes is that of the French sentry who shot down 'Americans' in uniform when they approached his post. They were, in fact, Germans dressed as American troops. When the sentry was asked why he decided to shoot, he replied simply that the troops had not arrived in a Jeep so could not be American! Another story is of Maj Gen Eugene Reybold who visited every theatre of war in his role as Chief of Engineers for the US Army and who said that he was first most impressed by the Jeep when he landed in England. He found that

The MB at work in south-east Asia. From 1941 to 1945 Willys-Overland produced 359,849 MBs, and Ford – under licence – built another 227,000

Go anywhere was the essence of the Jeep's success, with a low profile adding to its uncalculated benefit to allied troops in all war zones. At this time Willys-Overland had a work force of more than 15,000 at Toledo, Ohio

A communications Jeep passes an abandoned wagon and dead horse in France. The going must have been rough because, in spite of 4WD, tyre chains are fitted all round

A Fifth Army Jeep leads the way into Vergato, as it did into countless towns and villages in all theatres of war. Willys-Overland were already preparing a peacetime version

Is there a more famous road than this? This scene marked the release of prisoners of war who had suffered the most. It is reported that the sight of the Jeeps meant as much as the arrival of the victorious soldiers themselves

Lt Gen John Lee of the supply forces looked upon his Jeep as part of his personal baggage, even to the extent of taking it on trains when applicable. Reybold added that although there must have been many Jeeps disabled, or wrecked by enemy action, he never actually saw one that would not go.

The flat bonnet, probably designed to help keep the profile to a little above 3ft (1m), had other advantages: it was used as a dining table and also as an altar by army padres in battle areas. Two famous generals, Eisenhower and MacArthur, had a preference for the Jeep rather than more luxurious vehicles at their disposal.

Of that first operation in Burma, Col Claude A. Black recorded that as the Japanese swept towards Burma, hundreds of China-bound Jeeps stood on the docks of Rangoon awaiting delivery to Generalissimo Chiang Kai-shek. To keep them from falling into enemy hands the authorities turned them over to British troops and anyone else who would drive them north. 'It was the Jeeps' first whack at big-time war service.' The Jeeps slogged through glue-like rice paddies on liaison missions, pulled other military vehicles out of ditches, carried machine-gunners to the front line, carried women and children to safer places and, well dented by sniper bullets, carried on with the war. As the enemy drive was halted the roads were jammed with refugees and their animals and other possessions, but the Jeeps avoided these

Few combat units in World War II were more famous than 'Popsky's Private Army'. It used a veritable fleet of Jeeps in its strike actions. Here is the leader, Lt Col V. Peniakoff DSO, MC (with Pte Yunes Yusef Abdallah) moving house in Tunisia in 1943 (*Imperial War Museum*)

'Popsky' armed his Jeeps to suit his purposes. Here is one of them in action in Italy, complete with Browning machine-gun (*Imperial War Museum*)

obstructions by travelling cross-country.

A particularly impressive Jeep performance happened at the turning point of the war at El Alamein. Gen Montgomery was ready but needing some diversion. The whole story is military history, but Jeeps played a particular role in destroying fuel supplies to the tanks of Rommel. The Jeeps left Montgomery's HQ and, hiding by day, got well behind Rommel's lines. There they ambushed a fuel convoy with great speed and agility, using incendiary ammunition, and then disappeared as speedily as they had arrived, leaving a holocaust behind them. In the morning, when Rommel's tanks arrived, they faced certain defeat because they were without sufficient fuel to wreak further damage in combat.

An American attack near Aachen, on the French-German northern border, again used the Jeep's cross-country ability to best effect. Taking to the terrain, the Jeep crews on either side kept the main attack road clear for the rapid advance. Such was the amazing ability of the Jeep and — one must never forget — their crews. Many a wartime soldier possesses decorations won in combat, and the honours are entirely for their own military expertise and personal courage, but in their modest stories the Jeep is likely to be included as providing the means for their heroic actions. Hardened war veterans have been known to weep over the destruction of their Jeep by enemy action.

Thousands of Jeeps went to Russia, where their cross-country ability on the steppes and elsewhere endeared them to their drivers as much as to their Western counterparts. The Russians, with reason, called it 'Goat'. By the time the Russian advance to Berlin started, 80,000 more Jeeps had been delivered.

It is well known that Hitler's 'people's car', the Volkswagen, was put to military use for purposes similar to that of the Jeep. But, with the VW having only a third of the power, and in spite of good traction from the rear engine being over the driving wheels, it was in practice no competition, as mentioned earlier. The Japanese also failed with a version of their Datsun.

The Jeep was a great favourite with war correspondents, and one story provides a good summary of their feelings towards this remarkable vehicle. This anecdote is credited to the *Daily News* of Chicago when a Jeep with two correspondents arrived in India after crossing the Chindwin jungles of Burma and the Manipur hills. When it was pointed out that their geography was confused as there were no roads or tracks in the area, they replied: 'Shh! Not so loud. Our Jeep hasn't found out about roads yet, and we don't want to spoil it!'

A US Army Jeep speeds on a road near Mt Vesuvius. This was the worst eruption for seventy years. The allies set up emergency relief stations (*Imperial War Museum*)

Other Applications

From stories and from photo-files the manifold tasks for which the Jeep proved capable stand out clearly. There are pictures so numerous that they cannot all be included here. For example, the Jeep was used to haul a hay loader in wartime England, and to cut up waste timber to combat the coal shortage. For the latter job a belt drive was taken from a drum fastened to the right rear wheel, to a smaller drum with spindle drive, to a circular saw. During the war Willys was producing a Jeep at intervals of only 1½min, which meant that there were enough to divert to essential tasks which were not strictly military but nevertheless contributary to ultimate victory. The two examples mentioned are proof of this, for every bit of agricultural produce in the UK at that time meant fewer ships carrying food through the U-boat menace when, instead, they could be carrying the materials of war.

The engines which powered the Jeep were produced in greater quantity than any other engine of whatever size or purpose. They drove, or provided the motive power for, radar, radio, welding equipment, landing craft, lighting plants, and so on. In the South Pacific Jeeps, thanks to their low profile, could be driven through tall tropical grass unobserved, or at least difficult to spot and therefore to aim at.

The end of the day. Even a Jeep could meet its end in action. In this most famous Jeep cartoon by Bill Mauldin in 1944, first published in the *St Louis Post Dispatch*, the cavalry sergeant uses his 0.45 to put his trusty steed to rest

They were also used as locomotives when fitted with railway wheels. One Jeep could pull a train of 25 tons. At maximum torque this was at about 20mph (30kph). Fitted with a trailer on what might be called ordinary mud roads in combat areas they could move large quantities of ammunition as well as extra soldiers. The extra passengers would ride wherever there was a foothold. In Australia, American servicemen were pictured 'fifteen-up' for fun on an airfield. It may have been such pranks that helped promote a campaign against unnecessary misuse. With an official cartoon came the caption:

> To prove he's as game as the fliers
> Whose daring the public admires,
> Joe Dope hurls his loads
> Over rock-studded roads –
> And boy! is it tough on the tires!

47

When the opportunity arose comparisons were made between the Jeep and its VW counterpart. In this snow-clad setting the Afrika Korps insignia on the door of the VW seems a little out of place! However, when they were both put to the test it was a 'no-contest'

Another wartime task for the Jeep. Behind the allies' Fifth Army front lines in Italy a front-wheel version drives a wood saw for the field hospital (*Imperial War Museum*)

During the war train-loads of Jeeps like this poured out of the Willys-Overland and
Ford factories every day. More than half a million were built by 1945

On the right track? Many Jeeps were adapted to be used as prime movers on railway lines. This one, complete with a roll of camouflage netting, is also carrying heavy-duty oil in the 2gal (9 litres) cans at the front (*Imperial War Museum*)

With waterproofed electrics and a vertical extension to the air intake the Jeep was also known to ford through water with only the upper parts of the crew − and the steering wheel − visible. On one occasion during training the Jeep was used in a form of 'breeches buoy', crossing a river suspended by one rope and pulled by another. Another role was with airborne troops, who in 1942 trained in Northern Ireland. Not only could Jeeps be carried in transport aircraft but also in the larger military gliders. On the tortuous, winding roads in the hills of Sicily the Jeeps were in their element, for so much fighting power was packed into such small, manoeuvrable four-wheelers.

Jeeps bound for the UK bore at the back the words: 'Caution Left Hand Drive No Signals'. In spite of the other words: 'Max Speed 40mph' (64kph) it is doubtful whether any Jeep driver was prosecuted for speeding. After all, few cars at that time could cruise at over 60mph (100kph).

Passengers of Fame

It was probably not so much the popularity of the Jeep that prompted so many famous wartime people to ride in it as its versatility. At least

In September 1943 Egypt's King Farouk had an aerial view of the Nile Delta. Here he drives to the aircraft. Sitting beside him is his host, Maj Gen Ralph Royce, Commander US Forces Middle East. In the back are Alexander C. Kirk, US Minister to Egypt, and General Ibrahim Pasha Atallah, Egyptian Army Chief of Staff (*Imperial War Museum*)

This unmistakable VIP favoured a Jeep in spite of his disability. With (seemingly battle-scarred) Sgt Oran Lass at the wheel, on the left is Gen Mark Clark (then Lt Gen). The President of the USA was visiting US troops in Casablanca. Under the folded-down windscreen can be seen the American flag painted on in his honour

Another famous Jeep traveller, Gen Douglas MacArthur, characteristically smoking his pipe, in the South Pacific. It is thought that this photograph was taken in the Philippines. (Churchill and General Montgomery also used a Jeep to watch the Normandy landing operations in company with Field Marshall Smuts and Sir Alan Brooke while the navy was still shelling over their heads on the invasion coast)

the king or the general would not have to help to push it! Even so, to ride in or drive the Jeep had a certain *cachet*. President Roosevelt used it while reviewing troops in Casablanca in company with Gen Mark Clark. Montgomery and Churchill watched the D-Day landings from a Jeep on the beach while the destroyer in which they arrived was still shelling over the heads of the invasion forces. Churchill's daughter Mary drove one at a WAC training centre on Daytona Beach, Florida. In northern Burma Gen 'Vinegar Joe' Stilwell used one, while in 1941 an early model was tried out at Camp Holabird by the Duke of Kent (who lost his life in the war).

When US forces arrived in Europe in 1942 Queen Elizabeth visited US troops in Northern Ireland in a Jeep driven by Maj Gen R. P. Hartle, the troops' CO. Monty, after his victories in Africa and France, was driven by Jeep to a conference with the Canadian First Army by Gen H. D. G. Crerar, Commander of Canadian forces in Normandy. In its way, this was quite a tribute to the Jeep, for Monty mostly identified himself with his Humber staff car throughout his campaigns.

Variations on the Jeep

Official – and sometimes unofficial – Jeep variants began with the amphibian, originally designed by Marmon-Herrington, Herrington being famous already for his development of production Fords for war service. Herrington worked with Sparkman and Stephens of New York, a firm also involved with the DUKW (Duck) built by General Motors. The amphibian was built by Ford and designated Ford GPA 'Amphib'. QMC-4, the prototype, was on a Ford GPW chassis. Production started in the autumn of 1942 but the production target of 12,778 was never reached because the Amphib fell out of favour as a versatile reconnaissance vehicle. This variant was also known as the Seep, being, in effect, a sea-going Jeep. In contrast to the Jeep/Volkswagen comparison, the Seep, particularly on land, was not as good as the VW 'Schwimmwagen' which was more compact.

The Amphib was much heavier than the Jeep, by more than 1,200lb (544kg), so an extra leaf was used in each road spring. Empty it weighed 3,600lb (1,630kg). Maximum speed was 50mph (80kph) on land and 5mph (8kph) in water. A rudder was incorporated for water navigation.

A more important contribution made by the Jeep was as an ambulance. Soldiers are often wounded or die in difficult terrain, which is Jeep habitat. Ambulance modifications were made in the USA and also in the UK, Canada and Australia. The Canadian version provided a set of sockets mounted at the corners to take a tubular frame for double-deck stretchers, one by the driver and two above. Late in 1943 all Jeeps for British forces (now being assembled in the UK) were fitted with these sockets. In Australia Gen Motors-Holden provided conversions for use in New Guinea. Land conditions in the Pacific theatre were such that in many areas only the Jeep could cope with the terrain. The US Marine Corps also used ambulance Jeeps which were slightly different again, with the exhaust being piped over the top of the hood.

Another vital role played by Jeeps was with airborne forces. Several attempts had been made to 'compact' the Jeep for air transit. In England, Nuffield Mechanizations Ltd produced an airborne version using a modified MB chassis, other modifications including a steering column which could be removed for minimum height during flight and even a lighter steering wheel. Bonnet height was reduced by relocating air and oil filters, battery, horn and brake-fluid reservoir. A Solex carburettor was used and all possibilities of electrical interference were dealt with.

Ford produced this version of the Jeep 'Amphib' with production starting in September 1942. While production forecasts reached nearly 13,000 there were snags. It was withdrawn in the next year. Here it plunges into an ice-clogged river. A major benefit was that it had a power-driven winch which could be used to pull it up very steep banks once the cable was secured on shore (*Imperial War Museum*)

Driver, medical orderly and three stretchers taking British wounded from the battle at Caen and the storming of the River Orne. The Jeep is returning over a portable pontoon bridge built by the Royal Engineers. Caen was freed on 9 July 1944. British forces broke through on a wide front, while American forces to the west smashed through enemy lines in a co-ordinated offensive (*Imperial War Museum*)

This British adaptation of the Jeep for stretcher-bearing enabled four wounded to be carried prone. Also there was a spare seat for a medical orderly – although in this instance there obviously was not one to spare

In the USA Willys produced 'Stripped Jeeps' (Gypsy Rose Lees), and ultra-light versions were also made by Chevrolet (GM), Crosley and Kaiser (the last mentioned firm acquiring the Jeep in post-war years). Test results on these were not very promising and they never went into production.

After the MB had become standard it was inevitable that it should be used as the basis for vehicles with a more specialised purpose. These included gun carriers of both four and six wheels, and armoured scout cars. The basic attributes of the Jeep were also applied to heavier vehicles such as the ¾-ton, 2½-, 4- and 6-ton ranges. Many of these were dropped at the end of the war, but the original engine continued in other applications such as the power source for Signal Corps generators.

The US Marine Corps used a ten-seater Invader version for shore-patrol duties on the US east coast. Sand tyres on wider wheels enabled a speed of 60mph (100kph) to be used across the sands, but mechanical modification required only an increase of 3ft (1m) in length and a longer rear propeller shaft. The T13 gun carriage had a 37mm anti-tank gun on a modified chassis and drive-shaft system: an MB 6×6. By the war's end there were also ½-ton conversion kits which could be fitted in the field.

Tracks and half-tracks were also based on the standard Jeep, although not produced in significant numbers. Their purposes included crossing snow and exceptionally rough terrain, and uses as a

The radio in a Signals Jeep: strictly get-at-able, it was made by the Galvin Manufacturing Corp, in Chicago, to US Army specifications. (The British fitted their own sets) (*Ron Easton*)

small military tank. The US Army Air Force had a need for a search-and-rescue vehicle for use in the far north. The answer was front wheels which could be removed to take steered skis, while at the rear there were three-wheeled tracked bogies. These were equipped with 12in-wide (300mm) rubber tracks with steel cross-pieces. By these means the vehicle, fully loaded, exerted a pressure on the ground of only 2psi. Even so, it was not impressive enough to go into series production.

A more successful half-track was by Allis-Chalmers, designated T26. Based on one of the company's light tractors, it used the engine, clutch, gearbox, differential and steering gear of the Jeep. The final model, designated T26E4, won approval as 'Tractor, Snow M7'. This also had skis at the front, but the ground pressure was only 1.48psi. Painted bright orange for obvious reasons, it had a range of 200 miles (320km). When front skis were used the front wheels were held on the sides. Maximum speed was better than 40mph (60kph). For the record, all US Army half-tracks had '40' as the first two digits of their military registration number.

Other variants on the snow theme included the Studebaker M28 (T15) and M29 (T24) Weasel. Experiments were also made with what was called the T37, Crosley-engined tractor as an alternative to

This was the Signals version (note the suffix 'S' back left) complete with short- and long-distance radio and sprung aerial. The radio is mounted so that two crewmen can still get in the back if necessary (*Ron Easton*)

The Battle of the Bulge in Belgium. At the front, crew protection is aided by angle iron used as a wire-cutter. It was not unusual for the enemy to string decapitation wires across roads. The author's Jeep was similarly fitted in Germany later in the war and even after the war ended it remained fitted as some defeated troops would naturally try to 'get their own back'

traditional Husky dogs for pulling sleds, but nothing came of it.

By 1943 the Canadians had a need for a light tracked AFV (armoured fighting vehicle) for transport by air. Willys produced five prototype models with open-topped, welded hulls with Jeep engines. In this connection Marmon-Herrington produced a 'Jeep Tank'. This resembled an orthodox tank but without a turret. It was only 4ft (1.2m) high, and 9ft (2.7m) long by 5ft 5in (1.6m) wide. Only a few of either of these models were produced.

Mud, water and snow are the most difficult conditions for any vehicle to negotiate, even a Jeep, so other variations were made to cope with extreme circumstances. One used 'Mud Floatation Adapters' designed by Capt L. S. Rainhart of the US Engineers. These resembled open drums protruding at wheel-rim level, wider on the rear wheels than on the front. A rack at the rear held the extra equipment when not in use. These adaptors were a success. Experiments took place with buoyancy bags in 1943. In water not too deep to submerge the heads of the crew, the answer proved to be intake and exhaust extensions, coupled with appropriate protection for the electrics.

Jeeps for Peace

Prospects for the use of the Jeep after the end of World War II were considered even before Pearl Harbor (1941). By that time Jeeps already supplied to the allies had proved themselves in combat conditions. Any motor vehicle takes time to find its way from the drawing board to full production, so manufacturers have to think years ahead in normal circumstances. This was true of Willys-Overland under Ward Canaday. Canaday, in fact, employed an artist, I. B. Hazelton, to paint a number of pictures including peacetime applications of the vehicle.

There were twenty-four paintings in all resulting from the artist's co-operation with Willys engineers. An important aspect was the suitability of the Jeep for agricultural purposes. Other applications included snowplough, firefighter, prime-mover for pumps, and so on. Some of these paintings appeared in *Life* magazine in July 1942, but since that time the list of applications has mushroomed.

One of the first unusual non-military applications was reported from England with pictures showing GIs helping a farmer to pull a mowing machine, hay tedder, rake and loader. Stories like this were valuable to Willys-Overland in their peacetime planning.

Another story was from the South Pacific where Gen MacArthur had to guard against a likely Japanese attack on Australia. Needs included underground cables linking airfields miles apart without

Two of a kind – or before and after. On the left the Willys Quad, predecessor of the MA and famous MB. On the right the post-war military version, very similar to the wartime Jeep but more rounded, particularly in the wings. This was the MD-M38A1 in 1951 which continued for twenty years

interruption of their operational efficiency. Orthodox 'cut-and-cover' methods would take too long, so one Jeep pulled a plough to make the groove, another laid the cable from a rear-mounted drum, while a third levelled the ground: all of this was achieved at a speed faster than walking.

At the end of 1943 plans for the future became more clear. George W. Ritter, Vice President of Willys, was invited by a member of Congress to provide a prognosis for the civilian use of the Jeep. In Ritter's opinion, the military Jeep was not the answer for civilian use. There was no power take-off, the gearing was wrong, more effective cooling was needed for prolonged use in low gear. Similarly, other modifications were necessary if the low-gear operation occurred for long periods. Other changes included a larger diameter clutch to cope with the towing of heavy implements.

A realist, Ritter also pointed out that for the Jeep to be practical in civilian life a whole dealer network – with trained service staff and a full stock of spares – would have to be established. In other words, a rethink was needed before the Jeep was ready for the civilian market.

The US Department of Agriculture, plus state agricultural departments, were enthusiastic about the Jeep, to the extent of co-operating with universities and other 'think-tanks' to begin experiments to delineate the various aspects of the Jeep's versatility. These investigations were virtually nationwide, and the Agricultural Experiment Station of the State College of Washington went as far as producing a twenty-page publication called 'The Jeep as a Farm Truck-Tractor for the Post-War Period' by L. J. Smith and O. J.

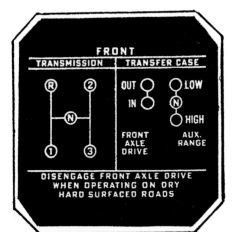

Each Jeep had one of these plates on its dashboard. The selection included English, Russian, Chinese and Spanish

Trenary. In this were illustrations of the military version being used for agricultural purposes.

Experiments were also made on the Jeep's suitability for tasks in forestry, ranching, mining and industry generally. Fundamentally, these confirmed the thinking of Ritter at Willys-Overland, with emphasis on the need for modifications to suit farm and factory. With all this research behind it, Willys-Overland launched its peacetime Jeep in July 1945. Reports of demonstrations were complimentary – the civil version was as suitable for its purpose as the famous MB had been for its military role.

The main changes included a special power take-off which could be

In 1947 Willys-Overland hit the jackpot on sales beating its 1929 record. Champagne flowed when the company reopened its west-coast plant in Los Angeles. The CJ-2A was the favourite, accounting for 65,078 of the total of 119,477 Jeeps built (serial numbers from 83,380 to 148,458)

The CJ-2A was produced for peacetime use when the war ended. Thousands of farmers used them as tractors and for many other tasks as well as for personal transport

The 1950 Jeepster VJ-3 was distinguished by a horizontal grille and there was a choice of 4- or 6-cylinder engines

M38 became the military version with higher ground clearance. It had 24V electrics and even greater hill-climbing and fording capability

used as a belt pulley or as a splined shaft for direct power drive. This power drive could give 30bhp, enough for virtually any agricultural task. This Jeep was the first vehicle to combine the functions of passenger transport, light truck, tractor, and power source. Apart from its many mobile uses on the farm it could be used also as a stationary power source, as its cooling system would permit prolonged power output while stationary without the engine overheating. On farmland it could travel with the same ease as the wartime MB. It could also plough, haul loads of hay bales or grain, pull a harrow, thresh, fill a silo − in fact do just about any agricultural task by itself, or as a tractor or power source.

Other changes from the military version included alteration of transmission, transfer case and axle ratios so that low-speed pulling of heavy implements or loads was possible, while at the other end of the scale road speeds of 60mph (100kph) were in order. There was a new combustion chamber shape to increase power, improved steering for sharp turns (necessary, for example, in ploughing), and a stronger chassis frame to cope with heavy tow-bar loads. Of course, military needs for armament stowage were discarded, but even with all these changes the Jeep remained the Jeep in appearance and general specification.

The name Willys-Overland has cropped up repeatedly in the story of the Jeep's transition from a wartime to peacetime vehicle. This is because from 31 July 1945 the government contract with Ford ended and the Jeep reverted exclusively to Willys.

The demonstrations to the Press of the new peacetime model on 18 July 1945 had been preceded by all manner of tests, with the result that the vehicles on view were anything but prototypes. In Florida they had been used to 'reap' grapefruit and oranges. Unlike conventional trucks, the Jeep was narrow enough to pass between the rows of trees and low enough to pass under branches weighed down with fruit. In the American North-west it proved to be the answer for forest rangers; in Arkansas it was ideal in the rice fields with their dykes spread across the irrigated land; and on a hillside farm the four-wheel drive and low centre of gravity had enabled the Jeep to plough in difficult terrain.

A. W. Wade, in his *Hail to the Jeep!*, describes a visit to a farm just after security regulations for new products were lifted. He watched a Jeep pulling a three-section, heavy-duty, spring-tooth harrow which in unmechanised terms would have needed three draught horses. Yet behind the harrow was a spiked-tooth type of the same size which would have needed two heavy horses. The Jeep was operating in low ratio for ten hours a day at 4mph (6kph). Some may say that as one horsepower is based on the pulling power of one draught horse this is

This Wagoneer is being air-freighted to England as one of a batch bought by J. C. Bamford Ltd, well known for their civil-engineering earthmovers, diggers and other construction machines. A 4WD vehicle would be suitable for those involved on construction sites, but JCB finally decided that they had enough work without building Jeeps under licence

Among the peacetime versions was this for the US Post Office. The rounded wings are a distinguishing feature

JCB put a Wagoneer through tests in England. It stood up well, but the vehicles purchased ended up as transport for company engineers

not remarkable; but in the soft going where the Jeep was working, power could be transferred only by grip – one of the great advantages of the dray horse and which the Jeep provided. A significant point regarding the Jeep specification was that for this type of work the Jeep was fitted with a governor on the engine so that sudden changes in load, such as might be caused by wheel-spin, could not cause the engine speed to go beyond an acceptable limit.

What was perhaps of greater interest in Wade's observations was the comparison between the performance of the Jeep and a heavy farm tractor on the same site. The two worked side by side at the same tasks and it was found that on fuel costs the comparison in the Jeep's favour was like the difference between feeding a shire horse and a pony. The Jeep also had plenty of power and never stalled, although its wheels might spin when those of the tractor did not. The farm manager found that when using the Jeep belt drive for other purposes, it out-did the tractor in power take-off. The ability of the Jeep engine to provide high torque at low rpm exceeded that of the tractor, especially in driving slow-motion machinery such as water-pumps. As for reliability, the Jeep needed no unplanned service or spares.

On another farm on Long Island in a potato and cauliflower area, but including beet, spinach, carrots, and so on, the Jeep had also impressed. It was used for the major task of driving a water-pump to clean root vegetables quickly for sale in the shops in Brooklyn and the City of New York. In addition to this stationary duty, the Jeep was used with success for ploughing, discing, seed planting and harvesting.

The Jeep is still of great value to small farmers for its versatility, and as an all-purpose buggy on the larger farms which now use more purpose-designed and expensive machines like combine harvesters.

Outside farm work, the post-war Jeep proved its worth for all manner of jobs such as continuous use pulling several lawn mowers at once — and at high speed — on golf courses, giving low operating costs and reduced man-hours. In remote areas they became the proven friends of nurses, doctors and cowboys. Because of its pumping ability, the peacetime Jeep became popular for firefighting, spraying orchards, and the like. An air compressor at the back made it suitable for paint spraying, particularly in outlying areas, and the belt drive could be used, for example, for shelling sweet corn. With a large 'follow me' sign it guided aircraft to their landing places, but it could also tow aircraft, baggage and fuel and be used for many other tasks involved in airport work.

Post-War Road Testing

During the early 1960s there was a possibility that JCB (J. C. Bamford of continuing fame in the earthmoving/digging aspects of civil engineering and internationally famous for his hydraulically operated JCBs) might enter the field of producing 4WD vehicles for rough terrain. Anthony P. Bamford has said that his father Joe and himself were considering a form of joint manufacturing with Jeep or manufacturing under licence. In the end, JCB decided that they had enough work with construction machinery, but during the investigative period bought about twelve Jeeps for evaluation in England. One of these, the Wagoneer of 1964, was made available to *Autocar* magazine for a full road test.

In the test report, comparison figures were given for the Austin Gipsy (which never really entered the ratings), the British Ford Zephyr 6 cylinder estate car, and the Land-Rover Dormobile. To include the last mentioned might be considered a little unfair as the Dormobile was a far cry from the orthodox Land-Rover, but the test showed clearly the qualities of the Jeep which put it out in front. On sheer road performance, only the 2WD Zephyr could match it, and in acceleration have the edge.

The 3,780cc Wagoneer (a large engine by European standards) could reach a true 90mph (144kph) in 51.6sec, and cover ¼ mile (400m) from standstill in exactly 20.0sec (21.4 with a load of 12cwt (1,344lb), (610kg)). The crunch was only in the fuel consumption of 14.8 mile per imperial gal (12.33 mile per US gal; 5.26km per litre).

At the time of the test Kaiser owned the Jeep enterprise. For the record *Autocar* pointed out that while 4WD and a high ground clearance ensured cross-country ability, the Wagoneer was exceptional in having the spaciousness of a large car and the high speed for cruising on ordinary roads. While this test car had a manually operated gear lever on the steering column (and a simple floor-mounted lever for high and low ratio) the model was also almost certainly the first to offer both automatic transmission *and* 4WD.

Ten years later, in September 1974, *Autocar* tested the CJ6, the direct derivative of the wartime Jeep. It was described as offering excellent performance at the cost of a thirst for fuel. Taking these factors in turn the CJ6 could reach a true 70mph (112kph) in 25.6sec, and the time for the standing ¼ mile (400m) was 20.3sec by which time the speed was 65mph (104kph). However, it used fuel at the rate of 14mpg (5.25km per litre) — which was not surprising with an engine size of 3,805cc.

There were two floor-mounted gear levers, one for the three forward speeds and reverse, the other with a to-and-fro action for the transfer case. From the neutral position it was back a notch for 4WD in low ratio, forward one notch for two-wheel drive in high ratio, and forward one more notch for high in 4WD. The cross-country ability was all that was expected from a Jeep, and a further compliment from the tester was the deliberate in-built flexibility of the chassis frame in torsion which, with quite low spring rates, minimised the risk of getting stuck owing to the spinning of diagonally opposite wheels.

In normal running, weight over the back wheels was at a minimum and therefore in 2WD (particularly in reverse) traction was not as good as some ordinary cars, but this was offset by the ease with which 4WD could be engaged and disengaged. The now standard 6-cylinder in-line engine with seven main bearings had a power output of 100bhp (net) at 3,600rpm, but maximum torque was developed at just 1,800rpm — 185lb ft (net). This gave the Jeep the endearing capability of trickling along at low speed even in high top for long periods if traffic density or other reasons made it desirable.

Selecting low ratio gave a reduction of 2.03 to 1, resulting in 3.4mph (5.4kph) per 1,000rpm in top — exceptional flexibility. It could also restart in top on an attested slope of 1 in 4. An extra which proved useful was a Warn electric winch at the front capable of pulling 8,000lb (3,600kg). When Dutch elm disease deposited an elm across a

Berkshire lane in the Jeep's path the winch pulled it aside with impressive ease (wire rope length 150ft (45m)).

In April 1978 another exhaustive Jeep road test appeared, this time of the Cherokee Chief. This was supplied by the British concessionaires TKM, who continue this operation today under their division Jeep UK Ltd. American Motors have retrenched partly as their earlier AMC Pacer failed to find favour in Europe.

If comparisons are to be made, then the Cherokee Chief competed with the Range Rover − in short supply from the time of its introduction. The Chief had the big 5.9 litre V8 engine, three-speed automatic transmission, 4WD with transfer case changing ratio in top from direct to 2.57 to 1, all of which having to be paid for in part by a high fuel consumption. (In normal use an owner would achieve just over 12mpg (4.2km per litre) although at 80mph (130kph) it would be only 8.8mpg (3.1km per litre)). The car was good for a true 90mph (144kph), had hydraulically operated tappets and electronic ignition.

On wet surfaces the Cherokee scored highly for its traction from rest, but, with more than half the weight over the front wheels, was described on corners as being like a ponderous front-wheel-drive car. The only other significant criticism was that in spite of the front brakes being large discs (drums at the rear) and with power assistance, the brake-pedal pressure meter used for testing went off the scale before wheel-locking.

4
THE MODERN ERA

The distinguishing features of the famous MB have been given in Chapter 2; the military version continued without significant change until 1950. For 1950–1 the only changes were a 24V system – the other extreme from a 6V – and the electrics were waterproofed as standard. Also the MC, M38, as it was designated, had a one-piece windscreen instead of the split screen.

From 1951 the designation became MD-M38A1, which lasted until 1971. The distinguishing characteristics included rounded wings at the front and an F-head rather than L-head engine. (An L-head is side-valve with adjacent inlet and outlet ports, while the F-head has overhead inlet and side exhaust ports.)

Although the Jeep was a Willys-Overland product it only became a make rather than just a model name in 1963 when Kaiser-Jeep was formed. Henry J. Kaiser was famous for the welded-construction ships so vital during the war years for getting supplies to European allies. He was also notable for his successful entry into the automotive field. Kaiser was later to become part of American Motors (1973) which continues the Jeep line of vehicles with Jeep as a registered name and copyright to them. So, during production of the MD, ownership of the name changed although the military Jeep did not. And in early 1970 the merger with AM took place so that the MD model Jeep was successively produced by three different companies, albeit still at Toledo, Ohio.

For civilian use the CJ-2A appeared in 1945 and continued to 1949. The only distinguishing features compared with the military version at that time were that it had a tailgate and, as a result, a side-mounted spare wheel. Slightly overlapping the CJ-2A came the CJ-3A from 1948 to 1953. This was very similar, having an L-head engine, 6V electrics, tailgate and side-mounted spare wheel.

Some innovation, contrary to the Jeep theme, happened in 1955 and lasted until 1964. This was the DJ-3A 'Dispatcher', unusual for having only two-wheel drive. An orthodox rigid axle was used at the front. It still had the L-head engine and was offered with either a soft top or rather unsightly hard top. The CJ-3B Universal Jeep rode the tracks from 1953 to 1964. This one had the F-head engine and tailgate but

MB Military 1941–5, the proven predecessor

MC, M38 Military 1950–1

MD-M38A1 Military 1951–71

CJ-2A Universal Jeep 1945–9

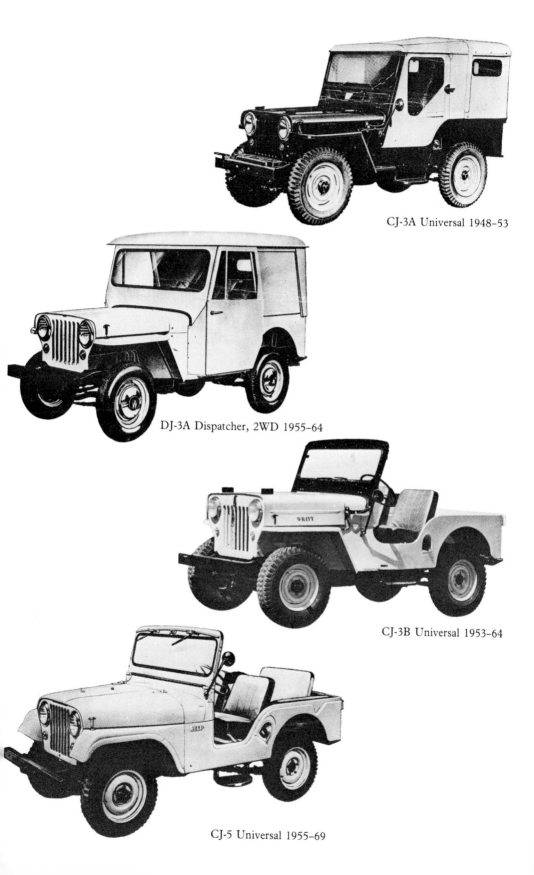

CJ-3A Universal 1948–53

DJ-3A Dispatcher, 2WD 1955–64

CJ-3B Universal 1953–64

CJ-5 Universal 1955–69

CJ-5 Universal 1970-9

CJ-5A Tuxedo Park Mk IV 1965

CJ-6 Universal 1955-69

CJ-6 Universal 1970-9

CJ-7 Universal 1976–9

C-101 Jeepster Commando 1966–71

C-104 Commando 1972–3

VJ2 or 3, VJ3-6 Jeepster 1949

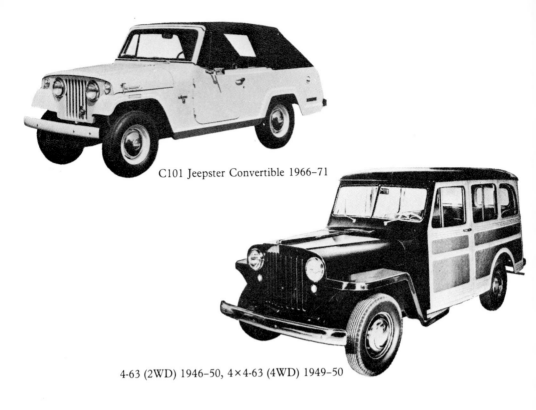

C101 Jeepster Convertible 1966–71

4-63 (2WD) 1946–50, 4×4-63 (4WD) 1949–50

6-63 Station Sedan 1950

4-73 (2WD), 4×4-73 (4WD) 1950–1

4-75 (4WD) 1956–65

Maverick (2WD) 1958

1413 Jeep Panel Delivery 1962–8

1414 Wagoneer (4WD) 1962–5

1414D Super Wagoneer 1965–8

1414 Wagoneer 1965–70

1414 Wagoneer 1970–2

1400, 1500 Wagoneer 1973

1400 (1974–6), 1500 (1974–9) Wagoneers

Wagoneer Limited 1978–9

1600, 1700 Cherokee 1974–9

Cherokee Chief 1975–9

1800 Cherokee 1977–9

Cherokee Limited (export only) 1979

FC-150 Truck 1957–64

FC-170 Truck 1957–64

2WD and 4WD Truck 1947–50

4-73 Truck 1950–1

4-75 Truck 1952–65

2400, 3400 Gladiator Series 1962–9

2400, 3400 Series 1969–72

2500, 2600, 4500, 4600, 4700 and 4800 Series 1973–9

reverted to angular wings. It had what European readers at least would call orthodox 12V electrics, tailgate and side-mounted spare. Overlapping came the CJ-5 Universal Jeep from 1955 to 1969, distinguished by rounded wings and some optional specifications. There was a choice of 6V or 12V systems and an engine choice between the F-head or V6. The wheelbase was nearly 7ft (2.1m).

From 1970 to 1979 the model with the same designation had side reflectors, windscreen wipers mounted at the base of the screen, rear-mounted fuel tank, 12V electrics, and a wider choice of engines from the 4-cylinder F-head to a V6 and V8. After 1972 the brake and clutch pedals were suspended, rather than hinged from the floor.

The CJ-5A Tuxedo Park Mark IV appeared in 1965 only. Distinguishing features included the F-head or a V6. This version had added chrome on the bumpers, on the hardware on the bonnet and on the passenger safety rail. Cushions and floor mats were also included in the specification.

From 1955 to 1969 there was also the CJ-6 Universal Jeep, the distinguishing features being a tailgate, rounded wings at the front, 6V or 12V electrics, side-mounted spare wheel, extended body on a 2.6m wheelbase, and a choice of F-head or V6 engines. The model with the same designation was manufactured from 1970 to 1979. In this case the distinguishing features were a 12V electrical system, rear-mounted fuel tank and a choice of engines from the 4-cylinder F-head to the V6 and V8. Also the wheelbase was extended to 2.6m.

During this period there was a considerable overlap of basic Jeep production. This overlap may lead to confusion, particularly among

79

those restoring a model of this vintage. This problem is highlighted by the introduction of the CJ-7 Universal Jeep in 1976, with production continuing until 1979. The distinguishing features of this vehicle included the option of automatic transmission with constant four-wheel drive. The wheelbase was 2.37m and there was more load-carrying capacity. It had bucket seats and a choice of 6-cylinder or V8 engines. The spare wheel was mounted at the back, and the 'top' was a triumph for all-round visibility.

The latest versions of the traditional Jeep come under scrutiny in the next chapter, but in the years between the war's end and 1979 one has to group models into 'traditional Jeep', saloon cars, estate cars (shooting brakes), and so on.

From 1966 to 1971 a current model was the C-101 Jeepster Commando. This also had four-wheel drive and manual or automatic transmission, and a choice of engines between the well proven F-head 4-cylinder or the V6. The C-101 was available as a convertible, roadster, pick-up or estate car.

After the C-101 came the C-104 Commando during the brief season from 1972 to 1973. The main distinguishing feature was a major one: instead of the vertical grille slats (synonymous with the great MB) it had a more lateral design of oblongs. It was more in the style of the orthodox car of the time with the front wings incorporated in the general bonnet configuration commonplace today. It retained bucket seats, foldaway at the back, and was also available with a half-cab or open body. It retained four-wheel drive and had the same engine alternatives as the CJ-7 Universal Jeep.

The story of the roadsters goes back to 1949 (only) when the VJ-2 or 3, and VJ3-6 Jeepster were on the market. They were spritely looking vehicles and promised to be a commercial success. However, they were fakes, in a sense, being two-wheel drive.

From 1966 to 1971 there was the C-101 Jeepster Convertible. The vertical grille pattern was used and there was a form of compromise at the front in which the bonnet covered only about half the wings. Four-wheel drive and bucket seats were included. The spare was rear-mounted, the soft-top looked after convertibility, manual or automatic transmission was available, and the engine choice was between the 4-cylinder F-head and the V6.

Between 1946 and 1950 there was an unusual vehicle with a typically Jeep front and a box-like estate car body. The model 4-63 was two-wheel drive, made from 1946 to 1950, and the 4×4-63 (four-wheel drive) during 1949 to 1950. Both used the standard 4L engine, but distinguishing features, apart from the body, were the divided windscreen and rear window, the latter over a tailgate.

The model 6-63 Station Sedan made a brief appearance in 1949. It had a 6-cylinder side-valve engine at a time when overhead-valve engines were coming in and even (with the Jaguar XK120, for example) twin overhead camshaft engines were in the offing. In spite of some exterior basket-weave trim it looked rather like a country hearse and had only two-wheel drive. For 1950–1 came the two-wheel drive 4-73 and the 4×4-73 with a choice of engines between the F-head 4-cylinder and the side-valve 6. The traditional Jeep radiator was replaced by a V-shape construction with chrome trim. The windscreen was two-piece; the body was of the estate-car type with two doors and tailgate.

For a much longer running period the Model 4-75 appeared in 1956 and continued until 1965. This had a similar but more up-to-date body shape and the grille was in the more traditional Jeep style except for a horizontal bar across the centre. Glass at front and rear was one-piece, and all had four-wheel drive. During the currency of the 4-75 there appeared, in 1958 only, the Maverick. This had two-wheel drive and tubeless tyres without a spare, which may have been reasons for its short life.

The first delivery van was handsome and sleek, appearing in 1962 and continuing to 1968. This had the first overhead-camshaft, 6-cylinder engine with the alternatives of a beefed-up engine or a V8. This had the traditional four-wheel drive and a squared-up radiator grille which was still recognisable as a Jeep derivative. In the same year, but finishing in 1965, came the 1414 Wagoneer, very similar to the delivery van in specification but with automatic transmission as an alternative extra.

Wagoneer became a famous Jeep model designation and still continues. From 1965 to 1968 there was the 1414D with de luxe trim inside and out, bucket seats, and a remote control, manual gear lever. Four-wheel drive was standard and the steering was adjustable for tilt. The engine was the V8-327 with four-choke (barrel) carburettor. The Model 1414 appeared at the same time (but continued until 1970). It was less ornate than the 1414D and began with an in-line six with two- or four-wheel drive. There were some detail changes during its life, but from 1968 it had mainly the V8-350 and four-wheel drive, both as standard.

From 1970 to 1972 the 1414 Wagoneer was identified on introduction by a new grille, reversing lights and side marker lights. Four-wheel drive was standard, but now there were five engine choices from the 6-232 to the V8-360. For 1973 the Wagoneers were reduced to the 6-cylinder 258 or V8-360. Distinguishing mechanical features were a mechanical clutch linkage and a brake failure warning light.

Models of the Wagoneer from 1974 to 1979 varied: 1400 from 1974 to 1976; 1500 from 1974 to 1979; and finally the Wagoneer 'Limited' from 1978 to 1979. All had V8 engines, power steering and tilt steering columns. Limited name plates identified the last mentioned, which also had cruise control, thicker carpets and air conditioning.

Another favourite Jeep model name — the Cherokee (still in use) — was born in 1974, continuing as the 1600 and 1700 until 1979. This had a grille of vertical slats, but, unlike the traditional Jeep's, was more like a row of teeth. This was a two-door estate car with tailgate, 2.7m wheelbase and energy-absorbing bumpers. A year after its introduction came the Cherokee Chief (1975) which also continued until 1979. This was very similar except for a wider track and cross-country tyres. Both models had a choice of the same three engines: 6-cylinder and V8 360 and 401.

From 1977 until this Cherokee series was suspended in 1979 came the 1800 Cherokee, essentially a four-door version of the other two. In 1979 there was a brief appearance of an export-only Cherokee Limited. Its distinguishing features were leather upholstery, extra-thick carpeting, power steering, air conditioning, automatic transmission and AM/FM stereo radio.

Pick-ups

Jeep pick-up trucks began in 1947 with a choice of two-or four-wheel drive (this pair had no model number designations). They looked much like the traditional military Jeep and had the standard 4-cylinder engine. They continued until 1950, then for a year as the 4-73 which was similar but made as a two-wheel drive vehicle. From 1952 to 1965 there was the 4-75 with V-front, more body mouldings and a choice of 6V or 12V electrical systems.

The FC-150 appeared in 1957 and lasted until 1964. This was the first of the modern cab-over-engine Jeep models. All had four-wheel drive and the 4-cylinder F-head Willys engine, but there was still a choice between 6V and 12V electrics. During the same period the FC-170 was produced which was similar in nearly all respects except that it had a greater load space and a 6-cylinder engine.

From 1962 to the middle of 1969 'Gladiator' became a name in Jeep history, with series numbers 2400 and 3400. The radiator grilles were more like those of the original Jeeps, but there was a choice from two 6-cylinder engines and two V8s. Loading was possible from the side or the back. From mid-1969 to 1972 these models continued under the same designations but with the 'toothy' grille of the Cherokee and an engine range extended to include no fewer than four V8 engines — the 304, 350, 360 and 401.

To see the decade out six versions came on the market with little designation other than being pick-ups of the period. There were three engine choices, a new clustering of the instruments, constant four-wheel drive, and loading from the back or from either side.

A standard Jeep for the public, 1981 – the Renegade, another in the CJ Series, the CJ-5. Note the roll bar for occupants' safety (in extremis!), the rounded shape and the wide tyres. Standard engine is the 2.5 litre 4 cylinder, with options of the new 6 cylinder or V8

The Jeep Today

Jeeps have had a tough history, being designed for, made for, and honed by war. It is therefore not surprising that the current 1982 models differ from their ancestors more in matters of finish inside and out than in major mechanical changes. The shiny exterior that pleases the eye today would have been unthinkable on the battlefield. Under the ownership of American Motors Corporation, however, the 4WD theme has been extended to models other than those bearing the unique Jeep name.

The Jeep CJ Series continues, and one can reasonably assume that it, or a counterpart, will continue for the foreseeable future. For 1981 there has been a choice of trim packages and power-train options. The CJ-5 Renegade is nearest to the old MB of military fame but there is also the CJ-7 Laredo with a hard top.

There is some confusion at this point because of different designations – and minor differences in specifications – according to the market involved. For example, there is the CJ-5 Renegade in the USA while in the UK the CJ-7 Renegade is on offer. The CJ-7 Laredo (pronounced LarAdo) is not on the UK market. Again, both cars are available with 2.5 litre 4-cylinder engine or 4.2 litre 6 in the USA, but

83

The CJ-7 Laredo 1981 has the same choice of three engines as the Renegade, but in both the V8 is not available in California. The standard 6-cylinder has been increased in efficiency and reduced in weight by 90lb (40kg). The weight reduction has been achieved mainly by greater use of aluminium. Four-speed manual or automatic transmission are options

only the 6 in the UK. Further, the US market can have a V8 – except in California. In essence, however, these are only local marketing matters.

The three main engines are the in-line 4- and 6-cylinder motors and the V8. All engines are now overhead valve with the following specifications:

1 4-cylinders, 2.5 litre, compression ratio 8.2 to 1, twin-choke carburettor, five main bearings, hydraulic tappets, and full flow oil filtration.
2 The in-line 6 has a 4.2 litre capacity, compression ratio 8.3 to 1, and is otherwise the same except for having seven main bearings.
3 The V8 has an angle of 90° and a capacity of 5,900cc, with a twin-choke down-draught carburettor. All three engines have an automatic choke for cold starting.

On the basis of power output the 4-cylinder motor rates as 100bhp, the 6 as 110bhp and the 8 as 175bhp. They are all low-revving engines, the in-lines reaching peak output at 3,500rpm and the V8 at 4,000. The in-line motors reach maximum torque at 3,200rpm and the V8 at 3,800 – all much higher engine speeds than the 1,800rpm for the earlier six, and the 2,800rpm of the earlier V8.

Taking the current list from the parent company in North America we have the fundamental CJ Series, with the CJ-5 Renegade and the CJ-7 Laredo having the standard 4-cylinder, 2.5 litre engine with the

84

This 1981 Wagoneer has a new front brake disc system with calipers which cannot 'bind', and the braking components are lighter, as is the power assistance

alternative of the quite light 6-cylinder. In most areas there is also the option of the V8. Next come the Cherokee and the Wagoneer, the former now offered with four doors and the latter in luxury form as the Wagoneer Limited.

The pick-up is available under the name Jeep Honcho, designated J-10. All these have the lighter weight six as the standard power unit, but the V8 is available as an option (except, as mentioned, in California). It is a handsome vehicle, its really functional role enhancing the appearance.

American Motors have cars on the market other than Jeeps. Their 'Eagle SX/4' deserves mention because it incorporates Jeep features such as the 4WD drive system. The standard engine is the 4-cylinder, but the 6 is an option. Standard is a four-speed manual gearbox, and all the steel is galvanised on one side. This two-door model is in the tradition of some of the best, sloping back, European coupé designs and is most attractive.

In some countries such as the UK Jeeps are handled by concessionaires (Jeep (UK) Ltd, North Way, Andover, Hampshire) but around the world are AMC's own plants for manufacture/assembly, sometimes in conjunction with a motor company like Mitsubishi in Japan.

In September 1980 the Jeep manufacturing facility in Canada was switched to the production of AMC cars other than Jeeps. In the same year, however, a base was set up in Egypt, and facilities also exist in Argentina, Brazil, India and Mexico. Large numbers of Jeeps are in

The Cherokee Chief for 1981. Strangely, an inside bonnet release is introduced for the first time on Jeep private cars. Exhaust emission has also been brought into line with most American state regulations

use in Turkey, but the numbers in the Philippines must be unqiue. Apart from the Jeeps left there from wartime, war-surplus Jeeps were delivered by the train-load, many becoming 'Jeepneys' — the word used locally to describe a Jeep taxi. Passengers mounted using a step at the rear of the usually lengthened body: poles were attached to the sides to support a light roof. It might be described as a Surrey with a fringe on top, except that instead of four seats the Jeepney packs in twelve.

The heavy and widespread use of Jeeps in the Philippines lead Sarao Motors of Manila to manufacture spares. Their range of spares, however, finally amounted to complete vehicles. Sarao then produced their own version of the Jeepney. Built on an extended chassis this was — and is — a shiny, splendid vehicle. It might be likened in its finish to the finest traditional gypsy caravan, with whitewall tyres and plenty of bright-metal glitter. Private owners of these taxis, used mainly for commuting between city and suburbs, like to compete in decorative features.

Northern Pakistan also uses the Jeep as taxi vehicles. Malik Idris Khan has recently written (for this book) an account which shows his long association with Jeeps:

Perhaps the most novel use to which they [Jeeps] are put is as 'taxis' in the far north of the country. These vehicles are generally old Willys CJ-5s, privately owned, and blissfully unencumbered by safety regulations of any sort. The usual load consists of eleven to fifteen persons with whatever

This is the Honcho pick-up with 4WD (which can be changed to 2WD at will). There are two choices of automatic transmission, the more costly having limited-slip on all four wheels. The latter is trade named Quadra-Trac

belongings they happen to want to transport; because the Jeeps are not modified in any way except for being fitted with beefed-up springs and dampers, the passengers usually end up perched on mounds of cases and bundles. Even more extraordinary is that the road over which these Jeeps travel rises to about 14,000ft [4,267m] above sea-level.

Before a proper road was built in the north a few years ago (as far as the Chinese border) Jeeps were the only means of mechanical transport in those areas. There is an air service to the north which is equally hair-raising but that need not concern us . . .

At present, right-hand drive CJ-7s, Wagoneers and J-20 pick-up trucks are assembled in this country. All are powered by the AMC 232cu in in-line six which, I believe, is no longer used (ie in the US and European markets). (Now the 258 which weighs 90lb [40kg] less.) All these vehicles have three-speed manual gearboxes and trim which is basic (very) even by Jeep standards. The only listed extras are free-wheeling front hubs. Pakistani CJ-7s have metal doors with sliding glass windows, a canvas top and side-screens.

Previously a CJ-5 model was produced which boasted a canvas top, 'doors' and side curtains as well as lengthwise rear seats (rather like those in the back of the Land-Rover wagons). Access to the rear seats was through two rather flimsy metal doors. This model was dropped in 1979, being replaced by the CJ-7, which also has the same sideways-facing rear seats, but not the doors in the back.'

On a more personal basis M. I. Khan relates his experiences in terrain holding a special challenge to the Jeep:

87

We in my family have been Jeep owners since 1946, and we use the vehicles for personal transport and odd jobs on our combination farm-ranch-nature reserve. Our first Jeep was a war-surplus Willys MB complete with trailer. The Jeep was sold in later years after several adventures (including one in which it was trampled on by an enraged camel – both Jeep and camel survived). We still have the trailer and it is regularly used to cart around a variety of stuff.

Later Jeeps have all been CJ-5s, and we have three at the moment: a 1962 Willys (US version); a 1976 AMC and a 1977 AMC, both locally assembled. The Willys has covered 210,000 miles [336,000km] from new and has been overhauled several times but still has its original engine block, head, gearbox and differentials, and is in everyday use. Of the AMC versions, the older one twice had to have a new gearbox fitted in the first 50,000 miles [80,000km] and the second one cracked a chassis member at 19,000 miles [30,000km] in normal use . . .

Mr Khan's last (and most recent) Jeep was considerably modified, but only to suit his own needs. In his terrain all his Jeeps were fitted with the heavy-duty springs and spring dampers.

To complete the story, China still has a number of Jeeps in civilian use. These are *the* Jeeps – the Willys MBs – and some CJ-5Ms (M for military version) – probably relics of the Nationalist Chinese Army in the case of the MBs and of the 1962 Border War, captured from the Indian Army.

So Jeeps continue around the world, new or war relics still mobile, and are likely to continue indefinitely. The basic Jeep had, and still has, a charisma pre-dating the Land-Rover and certainly the Japanese versions now entering the competitive market.

Jeeps for Fun

KOJ is the everyday name of an inexpensive journal catering for Jeep enthusiasts in the Pacific north-west of the USA. More formally it stands for *Keep on Jeeping* and, edited by Darilee Bednar, it is now in its ninth year. This is fairly typical of the great number of Jeeping clubs to be found where a state's terrain lends itself to cross-country fun at weekends. Some enthusiasts discard standard engines for veritable power-houses, and limited-slip differentials are widely advertised by the many motor firms specialising in any kind of 4WD transmission. Spares and specialised fitters are readily available (and one such firm is described in the next chapter).

The clubs' news bulletins are naturally similar to those of British motor clubs but with the difference that there are so many in the 4WD category. For example, cross the Canadian border from Washington state into British Columbia and you find a journal called *Backroader*, of the Four Wheel Drive Association of British Columbia. Membership of the association numbers no fewer than forty-seven clubs, every one of them in the same province. (First on the list is 'Back Road Bunch' and at the end 'Williams Lake Puddle Jumpers'.)

Much of the Jeepers' fun is in cross-country runs over strikingly beautiful country unapproachable by orthodox cars. If someone runs into trouble there are always plenty of willing hands, and expertise, to help. There are also races comparable with the mud-plugging popular in England in the 1950s – but for 4WD naturally more difficult. For example, at the Victoria (BC) Four Wheelers Summer Rally '80, the three-day event attracted 126 competing vehicles from all over British Columbia and there were more than 200 drivers.

In the UK budding enthusiasts wanting to restore a Jeep and put it up against competition would do well to contact the Military Vehicle Conservation Group (see Appendix I for the address).

As the author discovered when asked to judge a youngsters' model-making competition there is a good deal of Jeep fun involved. Indeed, complete models without a Jeep were so few, and the Jeeps themselves put together so well from kits of parts now available, that it was the excellence of the backgrounds – or battlefields – that tipped the scales. A prize could depend upon the realistic application of mud!

The Tamiya Plastic Model Company of Japan, makes a number of most detailed model kits. Apart from assembly and paint instructions each also gives a detailed basic history of the model. The famous MB is the subject of their 1/35 Military Miniature Series No 15, complete with a four-man crew and 12.7mm machine-gun. In No 33 of the series is the British adaptation for the use of the SAS (Special Air Service) complete with action photographs in the desert where the SAS became a new, highly skilled striking force. The instructions for this complicated model, having both twin and single Vickers machine-guns and carrying about fifteen jerricans of extra fuel to get right around the back of the enemy, also includes an account of the desert role of the SAS whose success prompted its continuance to the present day. Model No 43 in this series is of the Ford GPA Amphibian. This kit again comes with quite an amount of historical information mentioning, for example, the role of Marmon-Herrington.

5
NOW TO THE HUMVEES

In 1981 there were about 58,000 Jeeps in service with US forces, but no more were being ordered. It was felt that by the time these long-lasting ¼-ton trucks have to be replaced it will be the turn of the 'Humvee'. Detailed specifications were sent out to sixty-five companies early in 1981 and the race to produce a winning design began. It will be sad to say farewell to the military Jeep, but it is safe to say that it will continue indefinitely in the hands of private owners. Of course, new Jeeps will still be built for the civilian market. The age of 'Jeeping' will probably be with us until oil runs out.

The Humvee gets its name from the initials of its full military title: the High Mobility Multipurpose Wheeled Vehicle (HMMWV). Like the Jeep it will be a 4×4, but five times heavier at 1¼ tons. To make it multipurpose a common chassis will be augmented by various kits to convert the Humvee to weapons carrier, communications, utility, and ambulance. In this way the Humvee will fulfil the roles of four existing military vehicles.

A major difference from the Jeep specification is its diesel engine with automatic transmission. The Humvee will also have run-flat tyres and must achieve an acceleration of 0-30mph (48kph) in 8sec and have a range of 300 miles (480km) (cruising). Competitors for the contract have been told that they should assume working conditions to be 40 per cent cross-country, 30 per cent main road, and 30 per cent on secondary roads. As far as possible components should be from existing military or reliable commercial sources. Costings should include operational support so that the US government can combine purchase price and operating costs to reach a total life-cycle cost.

There are two phases in this new development, the first being underway already. This is expected to involve up to three contractors in an effort to deliver eleven prototype models each for test and evaluation. The winner is expected to get a minimum five-year contract, which constitutes the second phase. During the first phase government surveillance will be minimum so that contractors will be in a free and competitive environment.

The challenge to the American motor industry is formidable. They are to use their 'best efforts' − a nice understatement − not only in supplying the eleven prototypes, but also all the documentation involved, in training government personnel, supporting a five-month test programme, and providing the kits necessary for the Humvee's multipurpose role. Competitors will also have to provide test support including spares and repairs, special tools and manuals.

A front runner is, of course, American Motors whose Military Vehicle Division is claimed to be the world's largest. While the Jeep name has become civilian, AM still has massive design and production facilities capable of frightening off much of the opposition. However, the selection of the winner will depend in the second stage upon a procedure with four further steps, which means that AM will have to work really hard at the design stage.

The four steps used in the evaluation will reveal to the government the company's thinking behind the project, the depth of their understanding, the technical excellence and suitability of the vehicle, as well as mass detailed costings. The government will also examine the structure of the company, their relevant experience and track record.

There is a fascination about the problems of motor corporations meeting such totally precise parameters. In the four-step selection procedure limited discussions following initial evaluation are also forbidden. Gaps in information will have to be filled, yet the competitors will not be advised of deficiencies in their proposals as part of the limited discussions during step one.

The variety of roles for which the Humvee is the prime unit produces its own problems to satisfy ground transport requirements in the ¼- to 1¼-ton pay-load range, all with the same basic chassis. Among the eleven prototypes required from each contractor must be six weapon carriers and five derivatives configured as utility vehicles. The weapon carriers will include a missile system with associated hardware and a basic armour kit. One of them must also have a supplementary armour kit. The utilities must include a troop seat kit and a soft-top enclosure kit. All the derivative configurations must be compatible with all HMMWV system kits. All shall be suitable for being installed at direct support level, and within twenty man-hours at organisational level.

The kits/versions/components are all clearly defined in the proposition. The winch kit, installable at direct support level, will be at the front with a pulling power of not less than 6,000lb (2,722kg) on the bare drum (first layer). The breaking load must be at least 12,000lb (5,443kg) and a relief valve or shear pin must be set for 125 per cent of the winch rating.

The arctic kit must have the capability of being sustained by the crew. No external power may be used. More importantly, the kit will permit starting up within 45min and operate within one hour down to −50°F (−46°C). After the heater is turned on the cab must be comfortably above freezing point within an hour. Every vehicle must be able to take the kit which in turn must make provision for an operator clad in arctic garments.

The specifications make provision for a crew of four and seat belts. Two seats must be removable when not needed. Unlike the original Jeep the crew of the Humvee will be enclosed against the weather. A mass of detailed instructions is given for the carrying and operational needs of anti-aircraft missiles and their guidance systems, and also for the addition of basic armour and supplementary armour. These last items specify the weight and speed of rounds of enemy fire striking at right angles. When specified the fuel tank must also be armoured. The equipment weights for missile carrying are detailed down to those for the binoculars, night-vision goggles, combat rations and even the flashlight.

Basic items common to all versions are equally detailed. These range from a fire extinguisher within the driver's reach to necessary tools and a tyre pressure-gauge. Also included are a tow rope, tyre chains, tripod mount for a grenade launcher, pioneer tools mounted externally like the Jeep, jumper leads and first-aid kit. Storage space for the personal gear of the crew has its proper priority, and the weights are given for each item from bed-roll to overgarments, including hoods and gloves.

When specified, a troop seat shall be installed, permitting transport for six to eight personnel and their individual equipment. Again, these must be hinged to make room for a maximum pay-load. The Humvee must also be adaptable for carrying a shelter kit for electrical equipment and also mortar kits. Most kits are standard army issue so references are given to the appropriate military drawings.

There are many more complications in the design of the ambulance kit. Both the 'mini' and 'maxi' versions have much in common, including armour to protect both crew and wounded, and there must be provision for heating the patients' compartment to maintain at least 70°F (20°C) on both the normal version and that designed for cold climates. There must be no greater temperature differential than 35°F (5.5°C) at the inlet nearest the lowest patient and the exhaust near the ceiling. The extra heat needed on cold climate versions may be incorporated in the kit. Sound levels in the patients' compartment must be low, and provision must be made for visual and verbal contact between the driver and those in the patient area.

General illumination must be provided as well as focus type lights for each of the four stretchers (litters). Candle-power at 6in (150mm) above each litter is specified as is the lighting for black-out conditions. DC power outlets are required both for use by the attendant and also at the back, when the doors are open, for an attendant on the ground. The vehicle fuse-box has to be wired to operate the electrical lighting circuit when the ignition is off. The Red Cross markings must be easy to remove without damage to the underlying camouflage paint when this Humvee version changes its role. The specification goes on to list all the medical and surgical supplies to be carried, including racks for oxygen cylinders.

This is still not the end of the ambulance story. The two upper litters must be stowable when ambulatory patients use the lower litters as seats. There are many other factors such as ventilation, access from cab to the patients' area and an extension of radio facilities to the rear compartment. The 'maxi' ambulance must have – possibly in kit form – a full air-conditioning system. Apart from temperature and humidity there has to be provision for the introduction of fresh air when cooling is not required. The mini ambulance has to provide for most of the requirements of the maxi, but as the height is to be 23in (580mm) lower the design problems may be just as difficult. There also has to be a soft-top enclosure kit of canvas under which can be carried two stretchers and two sitting patients.

The armament mounting kit for the Humvee versions will include a 360° line of fire for three different types of machine-gun and an automatic grenade launcher. There are further difficulties with the deep-water fording kit. Assuming a full pay-load, the vehicle must be capable of going through 5ft (1.5m) of water over a firm bed. While in this depth for 15min, the engine must be switched off for one minute, then restarted and within another minute be mobile again. For the remainder of the 15min the engine will idle. When lubricants are drained afterwards they must contain less than 2 per cent of water or water-born contamination. After the water test the vehicle must be able to perform normally. The kit provided for fording must be suitable for the operator to fix, with special tools if necessary included in the kit, and thereafter be able to perform normally with the kit still attached.

Great advances have been made in run-flat tyres but, even so, the demands of the Humvee specification are daunting. One prototype – 1¼ tons, remember – will have to negotiate safely 30 miles (48km) of hard surface road at 30mph (48kph) with no air in at least two, but preferably four, of its tyres. In a fuel-tank test a charge of TNT will be exploded under the wheel nearest the tank (at that time full of water).

When it arrives the Humvee will have been well tested. No one knows who will win the competition, but the Military Vehicle Division of American Motors, holders of the Jeep registered name, would seem the best each-way bet.

6
RESTORATION

'No Jeep is ever beyond repair', says Mike Priscott of Wallingford, Oxfordshire, who has been restoring Jeeps for fourteen years. A man to agree with him is John Hendricks who has also been doing so for some years 6,000 miles (9,600km) away at Bellingham in Washington State. They have much in common including resources, enthusiasm, spares − or the ability to get them quickly − and above all know-how. Another source of spares in London is Metomat Ltd, who can also supply MB workshop manuals (the price at the time of writing is £5 including postage − but check by telephone first). The addresses of these and other sources of help and spares are given in Appendix I.

Anyone needing spares and likely to visit Paris should know about a source said by other enthusiasts to be cheaper than elsewhere. The name is GSAA (Garenne Surplus American Autos). In Belgium M Van de Velde is another source.

Mike Priscott states:

All parts can be repaired or replaced. The most consistent headache is body rot. Some people keep patching the rusty parts to no avail. It is easier in the long run to dismantle the whole Jeep. When the body is turned upside down the holes can be cleaned up and new metal welded in place. New top-hat section can be made and fitted, greatly increasing the strength of the body. Grind down the welds, add a few coats of paint and it's as good as new.

Priscott keeps a stock of spares so that he can offer a quick Jeep repair service. He says that he gets his mechanical parts fairly easily.

There is still a lot of stuff in the USA, France and Belgium. Some metal-workers will produce body parts to order. The canvas tops and upholstery can be obtained from three or four specialist suppliers, and the correct matt paint is now easier to get than ever before.

He finds that common faults with old Jeeps are poor clutches, ineffective hand brakes and leaking cylinder-head gaskets. 'But properly maintained and driven, Jeeps will last forever!' His own transport is a more modern CJ-6 which he has rebuilt from a write-off during a twelve-month period while repairing other people's cars at his garage. His final comment: 'I'd much rather repair Jeeps all the time instead of these modern tin cans; it's so much more satisfying.'

The outlook of John Hendricks is much the same. One difference is that he will work on all 4WD vehicles, but Jeeps are his preference. In his shop he has all manner of Jeep parts, including cladding to improve the rear corners of the body – an area prone to rust. When the author was looking around the shop he spotted an incredible 4WD converted Dodge produced for a West German owner. This was provided with extra high ground clearance, oversize wheels and tyres, specially mounted radio-telephone, and paintwork that was so good that Hendricks finally had to agree to show it in open competition for custom-built vehicles. The Jeep remains his first love, however, and his mechanics are provided with a flow of expertise on the jobs in hand.

Another Jeep enthusiast in the UK is Michael Turner, best known for his real vocation as an automotive artist. His Jeep was originally in Signals and is complete with the two-set radio transmitter/receiver of the time (one set being for intercom within a group of other Jeeps and the other for longer distances to report back from a reconnaissance position).

Michael Turner points out that one of the snags in restoration work, when total authenticity is the aim, is compliance with modern national or international regulations. For road use the Jeep must have at the back not only reflectors but also brake lights, and front and back must have flashing indicators. Also, of course, the vehicle must have civilian number plates. His answer is to use fittings which can be removed easily – for example, at a competition like those organised in the UK by the Military Vehicle Conservation Group. One method is to have indicators underhung, the fastening bracket remaining out of sight

Mike Priscott practises what he preaches – strip it down first. Here he has restored the engine and chassis before putting back the restored body

John Hendricks, in Bellingham, Washington State, poses in front of some of his spares. Behind his waist are roll bars for the personal safety of Jeep occupants. He is currently working on 4WD vehicles for customers as far away as Germany. The cult of 'Jeeping' also keeps him busy with tasks which to him are second nature (*Michael Clayton*)

behind the bodywork as each flasher is removed.

The British enthusiast should visit Warnham War Museum, near Horsham, Sussex. This is the brainchild of Joe Lyndhurst, another adept Jeep restorer. The museum is of modest size (as are entry charges) and for the record there is a pleasant restaurant in the main house. Where the Warnham museum differs from most is that once a month it has sales of militaria and on another day collectors' items. These ventures are informal so that anyone can book to sell their wares and potential buyers can wallow in nostalgia or find just the part they are looking for.

Joe Lyndhurst's interest in the Jeep began in 1942 'when I first saw a Jeep belonging to the Canadian Army, driven with tremendous panache by a young soldier who had volunteered to come 3,000 miles (4,800km) to help this country'. People at that time were used to seeing requisitioned vans and trucks that had been built for peacetime purposes, so the purpose-built Jeep was a sensation. By the 1960s, however, Jeeps had become scarce, and Joe Lyndhurst tracked down his first in Surrey. This had belonged to a hire company and was unscathed by military action. After a summer using it as a second car he decided to restore it to combat specification.

Restoration is much easier today, but it is of interest to the would-be restorer to know something of the problems facing his predecessors. It took Lyndhurst the whole winter to track down a black-out lamp, the correct body lifting handles, the staples for the axe and shovel, and the proper jerrican. It was also a matter of where did this fit, where did that go, and what was this for?

At motor rallies in those days the Jeep did not have a class to itself — not even a military section was included. Lyndhurst therefore had to enter the commercial vehicle class. By this time, however, other enthusiasts had gathered round in an upsurge of interest in preserving what was certainly the USA's greatest vehicular contribution to the war. More Jeeps were sought and the main result was a victory to be recorded in the Jeep story. As the 1967 season closed there were three Jeeps restored by Lyndhurst and they were entered for the London to Brighton Rally for commercial vehicles in May 1968. They were awarded first, second and third prizes for military vehicles.

The trophies were presented by Lord Montagu of Beaulieu whose national museum houses one of the world's finest collections of classic cars. At the presentation it was arranged that the Jeeps would provide a guard of honour for the arrival at Beaulieu of the late Field Marshal Montgomery's famous staff car 'Old Faithful'. The Jeep, felt Joe Lyndhurst, had now arrived among immortals like the Model T.

Michael Turner at the wheel of his beautifully restored MB Signals Jeep. The lamp visible at the front was for driving in black-out conditions, including night convoys (*Ron Easton*)

A restored Jeep still has to comply with laws introduced after the birth of the Jeep. These turn flashers comply with the golden rule of restoration — they can be removed without trace for competitions *(Ron Easton)*

All three Jeeps became well known and their appearances at charity shows, parades, and so on were in demand. This produced more recruits to the restoration task, although some were more interested in military vehicle history as a whole. All were prepared to give their time, however, and the result of this enthusiasm was an ever higher standard of restoration rivalling the most perfect examples of commercial vehicles and leading to rallies devoted entirely to military vehicles, with Jeeps as the most popular.

Joe Lyndhurst explains that it was far more difficult to get spares and missing bits and pieces in the seventies than it is now, and often the search for a part took much longer than the fitting. However, the increasing interest was such that the need was realised for a military vehicle museum with the result that the Warnham War Museum opened to the public at Easter 1976.

Illustrated is a Jeep which looks as if it had been bombed. This was found by Lyndhurst on a caravan site near Bognor Regis. Total wreck it may seem but Joe says that the spare-wheel carrier at the back was worth the Jeep alone. However, the wreck also yielded lifting handles (one can be seen rear left pointing vertically instead of horizontally) and the jerrican-holding straps, the bit which holds the tilt sticks ('tilt' being the word for the canvas cover for the occupants), and a large number of other parts.

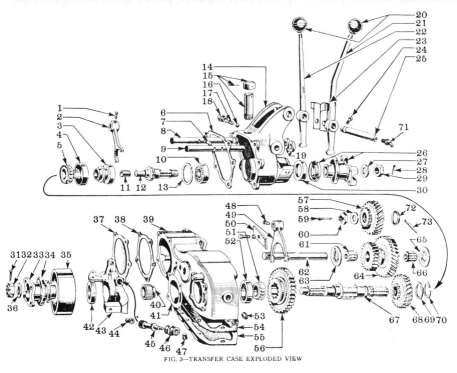

FIG. 3—TRANSFER CASE EXPLODED VIEW

A typical illustration from the Workshop Manual for the MB. This shows the transfer case providing low and high ratio as well as connecting front-wheel drive

This was found by Joe Lyndhurst not on a battlefield but on a caravan site on England's south coast. The number of useful parts reclaimed was astonishing. Items included the jerrican holder and straps at the back, lifting handles (one can be seen back left lying vertically), frames and locating points for the tilt (soft top) and many more (*T. J. Gander*)

One non-standard item can be seen in Michael Turner's Jeep — the flashing indicator switch below the dashboard on the left. This is a legal requirement but it is suspended in such a way that it can be detached for competitions in, for example, those organised by the Military Vehicle Conservation Group (*Ron Easton*)

A major factor which makes the wartime Jeep a favourite with restorers is that it is small, cheap and easy to restore. This is in spite of the need for aid from a good sheet metalworker and specialist treatment for the most common faults such as a crack in the block under the distributor, rusting under the fuel tank under the driver's seat, and rotting of the little running boards which had wood in them and which inevitably rotted with moisture and caused the metalwork to rust, frequently beyond repair.

When all the good parts of the wrecked Jeep had been used to restore the Jeep on which Joe Lyndhurst was working there remained the problem of finding a mounting for the axe head, part of the fittings for the pioneer tools fastened to the side of the Jeep. Enthusiastic restorers are by habit looking for original bits and pieces like this either for their own use or to put aside in anticipation of need by fellow members of their club such as the Military Vehicle Conservation Group.

As the Warnham War Museum resulted from pioneering restoration work one may say that today's restorer has it easy — and cheap. This is

Everything on this restored MB is authentic except for the civilian number plate (removed in competitions) and the 'flasher' at bottom left (hung so that it can be removed for display purposes) (*Ron Easton*)

mainly because of the ready availability of spares above all else, and also the availability of wartime Jeeps – mainly MBs, the favourite – through dealer-enthusiasts or from the hosts of farms where the Land-Rover with its extra comforts has taken over leaving earlier Jeeps lying around. 'Dealer enthusiasts' is a good definition as will be appreciated later in this restoration story, because nobody goes into the full-time activity of buying, selling and restoring their own or customers' Jeeps unless they have been bitten by the Jeep bug!

Despite some need of specialist assistance, a great attraction for the would-be restorer is, as Joe Lyndhurst said, that there are only six bolts that hold the simple body onto the chassis: two at the front, two at the back and two *near* the middle. The front wings (fenders) are bolted on, the threads are SAE fine – some coarse – and very few

On Michael Turner's restored Jeep the suffix 'S' stands for Signals. The white disc at the front was fitted for marking the weight classification for bridges — but whoever heard of a Jeep too heavy for a bridge? No wonder it is blank

spanners are needed. A socket set of $7/16$–$3/4$in will generally look after most of it although a 'hot spanner' (an oxy-acetaline torch) is sometimes used by the experts to free rust. The home restorer will have to use plenty of freeing agent and patience instead on any really stubborn bolts.

All Jeep restorers agree that it is best to strip the vehicle, including the engine. As you become a Jeep restoring 'buff' you will recognise some strange things. For example, many Jeeps have been repaired at some time in other countries with non-standard parts. The reason is that the Jeep is one of the most universal vehicles ever built (which in fairness applies to the VW) and spares that will fit are available almost wherever you go. For example, Joe Lyndhurst found that Jaguar E type front bearings were the same as the Jeep's. A good motor factor can provide just about everything in the mechanical line except body parts, although many of the latter can be produced by people like John Hendricks.

The prodigious output of the US plants could never have been achieved without the major factor of universal spares for the Jeep and the supply of the original parts to the production lines. The Jeep was also designed to incorporate as many as possible of the components common with other US military vehicles so that cannibalism would be practical on the battlefield.

A comparison is often made by older restorers and automotive historians between the Jeep and the early Ford tractor (which in England was built in 1917 in Liverpool before the Dagenham plant was opened) because the tractor could be decarbonised using only two spanners. Nowadays, of course, decoking has become a thing of the past since the 1950s owing to cleaner fuel and detergent oils, but a Jeep of wartime days usually requires the full treatment, including a rebore. Because of the ease of dismantling and rebuilding, Joe Lyndhurst reckons that a pile of three old military Jeeps will soon provide adequate bits and pieces with which to build one 'new' one.

His golden rules for restoration are total stripping, sandblasting and the co-operation of a good metalworker. One important problem is that US Jeeps have split wheels which let in water and therefore rust. In this case the answer is again stripping, sandblasting, but then metal spraying to make good. Nowadays there is little trouble in getting the correct olive matt paint for authentic finish. Lyndhurst finds an asbestos, eggshell finish the best from the two viewpoints of

The plum find by Kenneth Hart in 1975: a genuine Bantam from May 1941, and now a prize-winning exhibit (*Kenneth J. Hart*)

appearance and long life – and the eggshell finish is not shiny. He obtains this paint from Hughes & Bell of Manchester.

The total stripping mentioned earlier particularly includes the engine, for a rebore, fitting of new pistons and for new valves if required. Gearbox problems may be more difficult. Second gear and the rear main bearing usually give trouble. The problem is that when the rear main bearing causes trouble it is usually the casing rather than the bearing itself, so it is cheaper to look for a box with a better casing. This kind of fault is caused by lack of maintenance (lubrication) and once it has been overcome and the Jeep is restored then proper maintenance will keep it trouble-free for years. The spares are cheaper than those for a Land-Rover and the once-military Jeep is cheaper to run. For example, should the engine stripping indicate that attention should be given to the fuel pump then a spares kit is available (1981) for £3.60 which includes spindles, gauzes, and needle valves – just everything.

An example of the simplicity with which a Jeep can be assembled was given by the Royal Electrical and Mechanical Engineers during the 1950s at the Royal Tournament at London's Earl's Court exhibition centre. The Jeeps were CKD (Completely Knocked Down) which is normal when a vehicle is going to be assembled on a production line in another country. They arrived in crates in which were the parts, and the crates themselves had to be towed away as trailers at the end of the exercise. There were four teams each of six men. The sequence of events was as follows:

One crate top became a working platform (5sec); the crates were opened and first out were the chassis frame and wheels (10sec); four men carried the power unit as one tilted the chassis to accept it (34sec); next came the axle assemblies as the engine was bolted in place (55sec); axles were tilted while the wheels were fitted (1min 4sec); axle assemblies were fitted and hydraulic brakes connected with the rear wheels only (1min 10sec); six men lowered the body onto the chassis (2min 25sec); electrics and the cooling system were fastened while the oil filter was used as a fuel tank! (2min 37sec); the wheeled crates were reassembled and the Jeep started up (3min 15sec); the Jeep 'train' moved off – total time 3min 31sec by the winning team!

However, there had been some cheating by the REME crews in advance, apart from the use of the oil filter as a temporary fuel tank sufficient to get them out of the arena. Although this was known up to a point during the competition, Joe Lyndhurst found out some hard truths when he bought one of these specially prepared Jeeps thinking that he had a winner. Apart from the body it was impossible to make a real Jeep of it because of modifications made in REME workshops so that quite a number of 'pegs' were used instead of proper nuts and bolts — most of it was drop-on or drop-in. In spite of the modifications it was clear that the Jeep had been selected for the competition for similar reasons to those appealing to the restorer — the Jeep is small, cheap and easy to restore and reassemble.

Kenneth Hart of Wadhurst, East Sussex, is an enthusiast who bought his first Jeep in 1964 when he was seventeen, but who now has on average about eight fully restored Jeeps for sale, undertakes complete restoration, and also supplies or can obtain any spare parts, including items additional to the basic specification. To him the restoration and the provision of any kind of service for the Willys MB or Ford GPW is a full-time occupation. His story of entering the Jeep field as an enthusiast is representative of many others in many countries, and although his instructions on restoration are detailed — as will be seen — his early adventures show vicariously how lucky the newcomer is when compared with those who started in the early sixties, for example. He also has a precise knowledge of what one should pay for a Jeep today.

He started researching Jeeps in 1962 when under driving age and spent his weekends simply locating the vehicles mainly on farms where they were ending their careers. He obtained A. W. Wade's *Hail to the Jeep!* from the USA, but at that time there was little other information available and he found no military vehicle clubs. However, he did locate fifty Jeeps and eventually bought most of them. He found that cutting them up and sending the axles to the Philippines (no doubt for Jeepneys) was a good Saturday pastime. Soon military vehicle rallies started and from that point he found himself in contact with enthusiasts worldwide. A Ford Jeep owner in the north-east of England put him on the track of his target — an original Bantam Jeep.

Kenneth Hart toured the USA including the original Bantam hometown of Butler, Pennsylvania, and American Motors' works in Toledo, Ohio, without gaining much information. Even before then he had seen in Brighton the restored commercial vehicles, among which were the three perfectly restored Jeeps of Joe Lyndhurst. Hart claims that in the UK Lyndhurst set the standard for restorers which resulted in the Warnham War Museum. Of course, when a restorer starts from scratch and as an individual there are problems, some costly and others — on reflection at least — hilarious. Hart has plenty of stories, but the best one (which one hopes will not put off other seekers) concerns buying a Jeep from someone in Scotland, sending the cheque for what was described as 'quite a nice little Jeep', and being given the collection address in North Wales. He set off with a truck, and when nearly there found himself approaching what was little better than a disused hovel on a mountain top which no lorry could reach. He climbed a mountain track one quarter of the width of a Jeep and finally found a tin shed on wheels.

The Jeep was inside the shed and while Hart wondered how it got there he wondered even more about how to get it down the mountain as it was in very poor condition and did not even have brakes. He thinks that getting it down, often on two wheels, and twice nearly giving the whole thing up, took a year off his life. However, the same Jeep became an award winner.

Kenneth Hart is well qualified to describe the restoration process. Perhaps of prime interest is his outlook on price. In autumn 1981 he reckoned the price of a restored Jeep was £2,700 which, at a time of fluctuating exchange rates, would be about double that in US dollars. He has sold them to enthusiasts from 17 to 70 years of age and thinks that the attractions include the ease of working on and maintaining such a small vehicle and that there is now no spares problem. Regarding spares from France, and even complete Jeeps, he warns that many are Hotchkiss copies and, while cheaper, are still of lesser value as a substitute for the genuine veteran.

With his price estimate for the genuine article he points out that the price paid for a Jeep in need of rebuilding should be related to the figure of £2,700. That is, if someone pays £200 it should cost £2,500 to restore, or if the purchase price is £1,000 then £1,700 to restore.

His ambition for years was to obtain an original Bantam BRC40 as only about 120 reached the British forces from 1941 to 1942. That any should have survived U-boats, three years of war and thirty years of abuse in civilian hands was remarkable. His chance came a few years ago when another enthusiast, Clifford Lake, gave him some information and, after 1,300 miles (2,000km) of snowdrifts, breakdowns and other ill-omens he found himself the owner of what he (and the author) think probably the most interesting 4×4 in the UK. The illustration of this Bantam as he found it shows the depth of his dedication to restoring Jeeps.

As Kenneth Hart has now had so much experience in restoring Jeeps his detailed instructions on how to go about it are, not surprisingly, in line with the approach of Joe Lyndhurst and others. There are two important factors that the keen amateur mechanic should bear in mind. One concerns the costs already quoted by Hart, and the other the availability of skilled help. As the Jeep is such a small car there is no great problem in taking its body to a good sheet metalworker or its mechanical parts to receive attention such as a rebore, followed by new pistons. Here, it is possible only to describe what has to be done for proper restoration and leave the reader to decide his own approach to the job. His decision will depend upon his own skills and limitations as a motor fitter and what he can spend.

The restoration sequence by Kenneth Hart starts with the Jeep being jacked on to axle stands and the wheels removed. After taking out the six holding bolts the body shell is removed – the wings, windscreen, seats and bonnet. Sometimes a cutting torch is needed. Everything is then steam cleaned. At this point decide on whether or not to retain the set screws, for these may be cut off, or retained if the restoration is to be meticulous. All Willys MB ⁵⁄₁₆in set screws have AA or EC on the heads, but Ford GPW Jeeps have an F in the traditional Ford script. Hart puts it that Ford were very proud of their copy of Willys' copy of the Bantam!

The body should then be set up on a welding jig and repaired. Fabrication is usually needed on the front floor, the fuel tank well, both steps and all top-hat sections which rot because of the damp-gathering wood inside. Also needing repair at this stage will be the back locker floors and the axe and spade indentations on the driver's side. All welds are ground flat, and any buckling resulting from heat is also flattened. Similar repairs have to be made to the wings, front grille and bonnet (which often needs hinge repairs), and to the windscreen fittings which are of a difficult shape.

Taking the tyres off the wheels and splitting the combat wheel rims takes time as some wartime tyres can have 'grown into' the rims during so many years of disuse. When the combat wheels are dismantled a good suggestion is to discard the run-flat rings simply because they are so much trouble to refit and are of little purpose when the wheels are used with good tyres in peacetime conditions.

The engine, complete with carburettor and electrics, should be removed and also the gearbox and radiator. Virtually everything else should be sandblasted and carefully primed. Then it is time to rebuild the engine. As mentioned earlier, the engine block may well be cracked below the distributor as a result of frost damage and the crack may extend to the hole for the distributor shaft. This calls for specialist repair which, in late 1981 in the UK, costs about £35. When properly rebuilt the Jeep engine is a quiet, sweetly running unit, so it is a pity to cut corners by avoiding reboring and fitting new pistons. Reconditioning the carburettor, starter and the other ancillaries is also worthwhile.

When components are returned from sandblasting, the body shell parts should be finished to the top coat of olive green and all put on stands under a dust sheet. The chassis is then repaired as necessary and assembled, with reconditioned steering and new brakes. The road springs should be dismantled and reset (almost certainly by a specialist) to the correct centres given in the MB specifications. There is no harm in making the driver's side spring centres ½in (12mm) larger because there is more weight on that side – and it also carries the driver, of course. This modification makes the Jeep stand up well. When the transmission is assembled it is as well to put new working parts (Hardy Spicer in the UK) into the universal joints while checking propeller shaft assemblies.

Body assembly comes next, if not already done, lowered onto the chassis and bolted up. The steering should now be checked (again, see specifications). At this stage you are almost complete but the wiring harnesses have to be finished and neatly installed. Harnesses are difficult to make so the best plan is to recondition all the best parts you can get from broken-up Jeeps.

Apart from sources of spares mentioned in this book there is also in the UK *Exchange and Mart*, and by this stage in your work you will almost certainly have got to know other enthusiasts – and probably already be getting a good deal of voluntary assistance!

The price of a new, small four-seater car varies greatly according to national and local taxation, but the 1981 all-up price of £2,700 is less in the UK than the cost of a new Mini. The wartime Jeep, however, maintained with the same care and the know-how learned in reconstruction, should go on for ever. There is also the sheer fun of exhibitions and rallies, with all their camaraderie, and frequent requests for your appearance at charity functions. The communications Jeep of motoring artist Michael Turner has been mentioned, but Kenneth Hart points out also that there are many authentic components available for the basic Jeep, including – apart from radio – a carbine holder (which Turner also has), capstan winch, compressor, A bar, trailer, power take-off, winter top, windscreen cover and even a .5 Browning machine-gun with ammunition in the tradition of Popsky's Private Army. However, some of these items add greatly to the weight and proportionately reduce the power-to-weight ratio. Also, the Browning is likely to cause more licence problems than are merited by its possession.

Enthusiasm for Jeep restoration is understandable, but there is also the point that with the coming of the Humvee and the end of the road for the military Jeep, well-restored examples will surely never depreciate. Transport of incalculable value to the successful conclusion of World War II included the Liberty Ships built by Kaiser (later to take over Willys as events proved), the ubiquitous Dakota, and the immortal Hurricane and Spitfire. The only land vehicle to rank with these was the Jeep.

APPENDIX I

Sources of Help and Spares

GSAA (Garenne Surplus American Autos), 99 Rue de l'Aigle, 92250 La Garenne, Colombes, Paris, France

Hart, Kenneth J., Cottenden Road, Stonegate, Wadhurst, East Sussex TB5 7DX

Hendricks, John, North-West Off-Road Specialties, 1990 Iowa Street, Bellingham, Washington 98225, USA

Metomat Ltd, Daleham Mews, London NW3 (Tel: 01-435 8231)

Military Vehicle Conservation Group, 10 Thames Mead, Crowmarsh, Oxfordshire

Priscott, Michael, Goldfinch Lane, Wallingford, Oxfordshire (Tel: 0491-651481)

Van de Velde, M, Allée le Cavalier 2, 1474 Ways, près de Waterloo, Belgium

Warnham War Museum, Nr Horsham, West Sussex (Tel: 0403-65607)

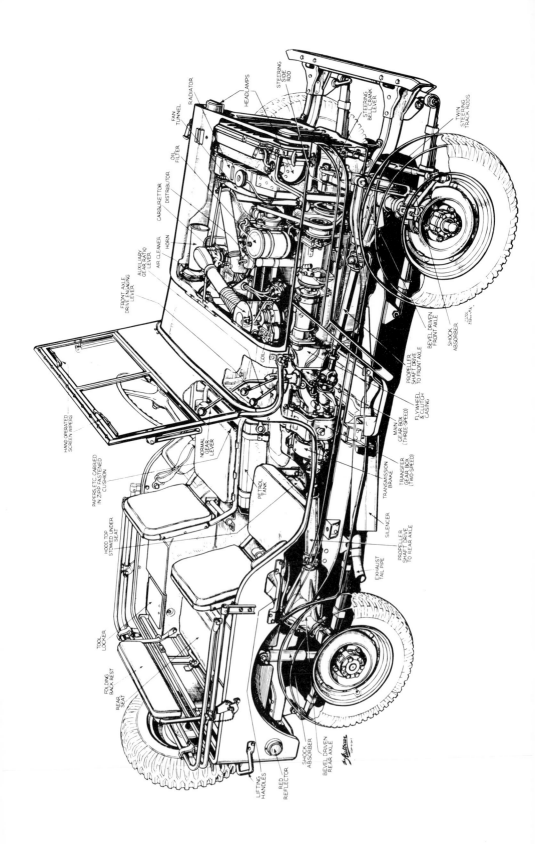

HAND OPERATED
SCREEN WIPERS

PAPERS, ETC. CARRIED
IN ZIPP FASTENED
CUSHION

HOOD TOP
STOWED UNDER
SEAT

TOOL
LOCKER

FOLDING
BACK REST

REAR
SEAT

LIFTING
HANDLES

RED
REFLECTOR

SHOCK
ABSORBER

BEVEL DRIVEN
REAR AXLE

EXHAUST
TAIL PIPE

PROPELLER
SHAFT DRIVE
TO REAR AXLE

SILENCER

TRANSMISSION
BRAKE

TRANSFER
GEAR BOX
(TWO SPEED)

MAIN
GEAR BOX
(THREE SPEED)

FLYWHEEL
& CLUTCH
CASING

PROPELLER
SHAFT DRIVE
TO FRONT AXLE

SHOCK
ABSORBER

BEVEL DRIVEN
FRONT AXLE

TWIN
STEERING
TRACK RODS

STEERING
BELL CRANK
LEVER

STEERING
SIDE
ROD

HEADLAMPS

RADIATOR

FAN
TUNNEL

OIL
FILTER

DISTRIBUTOR

CARBURETTOR

HORN

AIR CLEANER

AUXILIARY
GEAR RATIO
LEVER

FRONT AXLE
DRIVE ENGAGING
LEVER

NORMAL
GEAR
LEVER

PETROL
TANK

APPENDIX II

MB Specification Summary

Engine

Willys model 441 or 442 'Go Devil' 4-cylinder in-line water-cooled side-valve (L-head) petrol (gasoline) engine, developing 60bhp (54 net) at 4,000rpm and a max torque of 105lb ft (95 net) at 2,000rpm. Cubic capacity 134.2cu in (2,199cc). Bore and stroke 3.125×4.375in (79.375×111.125mm). Compression ratio 6.48:1. SAE and RAC rated hp: 15.63. Firing order 1-3-4-2. Valve tappet clearance (cold), inlet and exhaust: 0.014in. Spark plugs: 14mm Champion QM2 or Auto-Lite AN7, gap 0.030in. Auto-Lite ignition distributor (dustproof on certain vehicles), contact breaker gap: 0.020in. AC model AF mechanical fuel pump. Carter model WO-539S down-draught carburettor.

Note: Ford-built engines were virtually identical but used studs instead of bolts for connecting rod bearing caps; rods were interchangeable.

Transmission

Borg and Beck model 11123 single dry-plate clutch; driven plate diameter 7⅞in.* Warner Gear model T-84-J gearbox with three forward speeds and one reverse; synchromesh on second and top gear. Spicer or Brown-Lipe transfer case/auxiliary gearbox bolted on to main gearbox, with high (direct) and low (1.97) range. Separate lever to engage or disengage front-wheel drive. Locking arrangement to prevent use of low transfer ratio with rear-wheel drive only. Provision for PTO (power take-off) at rear end of gearbox mainshaft. Spicer U-jointed propeller shafts to front and rear axles. Spicer fully floating driving axles with Bendix-Weiss, Rzeppa, Spicer or Tracta constant-velocity joints.

Gear Ratios

	Gearbox	Overall High Range	Overall Low Range
First	2.665	13.005	25.573
Second	1.564	7.632	15.036
Top	1.000	4.880	9.614
Reverse	3.554	17.344	34.167

Chassis

Midland Steel ladder-type chassis frame (with differences in front cross member and shock-absorber mountings between Ford and Willys). Parabolic leaf springs, front and rear with 'U' shackles and screwed bushes. Rear spring assemblies identical left and right. Left-hand front spring had different spring rate from right-hand spring to cope with extra load (engine offset to left) and was identified by letter 'L' painted in yellow on underside. Willys from s/n 146774 and all Fords were fitted with torque reaction stabiliser spring below left-hand front spring (could also be fitted on earlier Willys vehicles). Hydraulic telescopic shock absorbers. Bendix hydraulic service brakes on all wheels. Mechanical parking brake on transfer case output shaft (externally contracting on most, internally expanding on some late production models).

Ross cam and twin-lever steering gear. Split-rim combat-type road wheels (conventional single-piece type on early models) with 6.00 × 16/6-ply tyres, usually with non-directional cross-country tread. Tyre pressures, front and rear: 30–35psi.

Dimensions and Weights

Wheelbase: 80in. Track (tread), front and rear: 48¼in (49in with combat wheels). Overall length: 131in (early models 132¼–132¾in). Overall width: 62in. Overall height (with normal load), at cowl: 40in, at top of steering wheel: 51¼–52in, with top up: 72in (early models 69¾in). Ground clearance 8¾in. Shipping weight (less fuel, water): 2,337lb. Kerb weight of complete vehicle: 2,453lb (early models 2,315lb). Gross vehicle weight, off highway: 3,253lb, on highway: 3,653lb. Maximum payload: 800lb. Maximum trailed load: 1,000lb.

Electrical

6V negative earth system. Sealed-beam headlights, mounted on hinged brackets. Lighting system controlled by black-out (main) light switch on dashboard (later production models had rotary-type light switch, replacing push-pull type). Auto-Lite generator, regulator and starter motor. The spring-loaded generator brace could be pulled up to slacken the fan belt, thus preventing the fan from throwing water over the engine when fording.

A radio outlet box was fitted against the body side panel adjacent to the right front seat on later vehicles. Certain vehicles were fitted with a 12V 55A auxiliary generator, V-belt-driven from the transmission power take-off.

* The use of fractions follows original specifications.

Detailed Specifications

Engine

Type   **L Head**

Number of cylinders	4
Bore	$3\frac{1}{8}$in
Stroke	$4\frac{3}{8}$in
Piston displacement	134.2cu in
Compression ratio	6.48 to 1
Output, max	60bhp at 4000rpm
Rating, SAE	15.63hp
Compression	111lb at 185rpm
Torque, max	105lb ft at 2000rpm
Firing order	1-3-4-2

Cylinder block

Bore size	3.125–.127in

Cylinder head torque settings

Cylinder head screw	65–75lb ft
Cylinder head stud nut	60–5lb ft

Crankshaft

Counterweights	4

Crankshaft main bearings

Bearing journals	3
Front	2.3340×1.920in
Centre	$2.3340 \times 1\frac{13}{16}$in
Rear	$2.3340 \times 1\frac{3}{4}$in
Thrust	front
End-play	0.004–006in
Bearing clearance	0.001in
Type	Steel back, babbitt lined
Non-adjustable	
Replaceable without reaming	
Torque settings	65–70lb ft

Connecting rod

Centre-to-centre length	$9\frac{3}{16}$in
Upper end	Piston pin locked in rod

Lower bearing type
  Steel back, babbitt lined, replaceable

Lower bearing diameter and length
                       $1\frac{15}{16} \times 1\frac{5}{16}$in

Clearance on crankshaft	0.0008–0023in
Side clearance	0.005–009in
Torque settings	50–5lb ft
Installation	from top

Offset away from nearest main bearing
  Oil spray hole away from camshaft

Piston

Lo-Ex Lynite T-slot, oval ground, tin plated

Length	$3\frac{3}{4}$in
Clearance top land	0.0205–0225in
Clearance skirt	0.003in

Oversize piston available
        0.010in, 0.020in, 0.030in

Number rings	3
Compression ring	2 width $\frac{3}{32}$in
Oil ring	1 width $\frac{3}{16}$in
Ring gap	0.008–013in

Ring-to-groove clearance
                0.0005–0015in

Piston pin hole
  Diamond bored
       $\frac{13}{16} \times 0.8007–0.8119$in

Piston pin

Length	$2\frac{25}{32}$in
Diameter	$1\frac{3}{16}$in
Type	Locked-in-rod
Clearance in piston	0.0001–0005in

Camshaft

Number of bearings	4

Bearing journal diameter

Front	$2\frac{5}{16}$in
Front intermediate	$2\frac{1}{4}$in
Rear intermediate	$2\frac{3}{16}$in
Rear	$1\frac{3}{4}$in
Thrust taken	Front
End play control	Plunger and spring

Camshaft bearings

Front	Steel back babbitt lined
Clearance	0.002–0035in

Intake valve

Tappet clearance cold	0.014in
Seat angle	45deg
Diameter head	$1\frac{17}{32}$in
Length overall	$5\frac{3}{4}$in
Stem diameter	0.373in

Stem-to-guide clearance
                0.0015–0.00325in

Intake opens
  9deg BTC flywheel (0.039in piston travel)

Intake closes
  50deg ABC flywheel (3.772in piston travel)

Lift	$2\frac{3}{64}$in

Exhaust valve

Tappet clearance cold	0.014in
Seat angle	45deg
Diameter head	$1\frac{15}{32}$in
Length overall	$5\frac{3}{4}$in
Stem diameter	0.3725in
Stem-to-guide clearance	0.002–0375in

Exhaust opens
  47deg BBC flywheel (3.799in piston travel)

Exhaust closes
12deg ATC flywheel (0.054in piston travel)
Lift   23⁄64in

Valve spring
Free length   2½in
Spring pressure valve closed
    50lb length 27⁄64in
Spring pressure valve open
    116lb length 1¾in
Closed coil end of spring
    Installed up against block

Valve tappet
Overall length   27⁄8in
Stem diameter   0.6240–0.6245in
Clearance to guide   0.0005–0.002in
Adjusting screw   3⁄8in–24 thread × 1⁄32in

Timing chain
Link belt
Number links   47
Width   1.0in
Pitch   ½in
Type   Non-adjustable

Fan belt
Type   'V'
Angle of V   42deg
Length outside   44⅛in
Width   11⁄16in

Oil pump
Type   Planetary gear
Driven from camshaft   Gear

Oil pressure relief
Pressure   40psi actual–75psi gauge at 30mph
Adjustable   Shims in spring retainer
Oil filter   Purolator No 27078

Fuel System
Carburettor
Make   Carter
Model   WO-539 S
Flange   1.0in
Primary venturi diameter   11⁄32in
Main venturi diameter   1.0in
Float setting   3⁄8in

Fuel intake
Square vertical spring loaded Needle
    No 53 drill size in needle seat
Fuel line Connection
    1⁄8in pipe thread–3⁄16in inverted flared tube elbow

Low speed jet tube
Jet size   No 71 drill
Idle well jet   No 61 drill
Idle screw seat   No 46 drill
Main nozzle discharge jet diameter
    0.096in
Metering rod   No 75–547
Jet size (diameter)   0.070in
Setting (use gauge No T-109-26)
    2.718in
Accelerating pump
Discharge jet   No 73 drill
Intake ball check   No 40 drill
Discharge disc check   No 40 drill
Relief passage to outside   No 42 drill
Adjustment (use gauge
    T-109-117 S)   17⁄64in

Air cleaner
Make   Oakes
Model   613300
Type   Oil bath

Fuel pump
Make   AC
Model   AF
Type   Camshaft
Pressure
    1½–2½lb at 16in above outlet at 1800rpm

Fuel tank
Make   Willys
Location   Under driver's seat
Filler cap   AC No 850018

Fuel filter
Make   AC
Model   T-2
Type   Disc
Mounting   Mounted on dash

Cooling System
Cooling capacity   11 US qt
Radiator   Jamestown
Radiator filler cap   AC
Fan 4-blade 15in diameter   Hayes
Fan belt
Type   'V'
Length outside   44⅛in
Width   11⁄16in
Angle of V   42 deg
Water pump
Type   Centrifugal
Location   Front of cylinder block

Drive   Belt

Bearing

    Permanently sealed-lubricated ball

Thermostat

Location

    Water outlet top cylinder head

Starts to open at   145–155deg

Fully open   170deg

Anti-freeze (US measures)

Temp °F	Alcohol, Qts	Ethylene Glycol, Qts	Temp °C
30	1	1	−1.1
20	2⅛	2	−6.6
10	3¼	3	−12.2
0	4¼	3¾	−17.7
−10	5	4½	−23
−20	5½	4¾	−29
−30	6¾	5½	−34
−40	7¼	6	−40

(To convert quantities into imperial quarts multiply by 0.833. To convert quantities into metric litres multiply by 0.946.)

Clutch

Type   Single, dry plate

Driven plate

Make   Borg & Beck 1123

Size   7⅞in

Facings

    1 woven and 1 moulded asbestos

    Diameter   Inside 5⅛in; outside 7⅞in

    Thickness   ⅛in (0.125in)

    Torque capacity   132lb ft

Pressure plate

Make   Atwood

Number springs   3

Spring pressure at 1⁹⁄₁₆in   220–30lb

Clutch release bearing

Type

    Sealed ball-bearing – pre-lubricated

Clutch shaft bushing

Location   In crankshaft

Material   Bronze bushing

    (impregnated with graphite)

Size, inside diameter   0.628in

Clutch pedal

Adjustment ¾in free pedal travel before release bearing contacts clutch fingers

Transfer Case

Transfer case

Make   Spicer

Model   18

Mounting   Unit with transmission

Shift lever   Floor

Ratio   High 1:1

                    Low 1.97:1

Transfer case bearings

Transmission mainshaft   Ball

Idler gear   2 roller

Output shaft   Taper roller

Front axle clutch shaft

    Front bearing   Ball

    Rear pilot in output shaft

         Bronze bushing ID 0.627in

Transfer case oil

Capacity   3 US pt

Grade (usually)   SAE 90

Speedometer drive

Drive gear teeth   4

Driven gear teeth   14

Propeller Shaft and Universal Joints

Propeller shaft

Make   Spicer

Shaft diameter   1¼in

Length (front) (joint centre to centre)

                        21¹¹⁄₁₆in

Length (rear) (joint centre to centre)

                       20 ¹⁄₃₂in

Universal joint front drive   Front

Make   Spicer

Type   U-bolt and snap ring

Model   1268

Bearings   Needle roller Spicer 98–851

Universal joint front drive   Rear

Make   Spicer

Type   Snap ring and U-bolt

Model   1261

Bearings   Needle roller Spicer 98–851

Universal joint rear drive   Front

Make   Spicer

Type   Snap ring slip joint

Model   1261

Bearings   Needle roller Spicer 98–851

Universal joint rear drive   Rear

Make   Spicer

Type   U-bolt and snap rings

Model 1268
Bearings   Needle roller Spicer 98–851

Steering
Steering gear
Make	Ross
Type	Cam and twin pin lever
Model	T-12
Ratio	Variable ratio 14-12-14 to 1
Wheel	3 spoke 17¼in safety type

Bearings
Cam upper	Ball
Cam lower	Ball
Lever shaft	Bushing
Steering column upper	Ball

Lever shaft
Clearance to bushing 0.0005–0.0025in
Steering connecting rod
Make	Colombus Auto Parts
Type	Spring loaded
Adjustment	Threaded plug

Steering geometry
Toe-in	³⁄₆₄–³⁄₃₂in
Camber	1½deg
Caster	3deg
Toe out	
Inside wheel	20deg
Outside wheel	19deg 45ft

Front Axle
Make	Spicer
Drive	Through springs
Type	Full floating
Road clearance	8⁷⁄₁₆in

Differential (same as rear axle)
Drive	Hypoid
Gear ratio	4.88:1
Bearings	Timken roller
Oil capacity	2½ US pt
Adjustment	Shims
Gears (pinion)	2

Steering knuckle thrust
Adjusted by shims, should have 25–35in lb pull without oil seal assembly in position
Steering knuckle
Bearings upper and lower
Timken roller
Turning arc   26deg

Tie rods
Number	2
Right-hand length centre-to-centre	24¼in
Left-hand length centre-to-centre	17¹¹⁄₃₂in
Tie rod ends	Serviced as a unit

Steering geometry
King pin inclination	7½deg
Wheel camber	1½deg
Wheel caster	3deg
Wheel toe-in	³⁄₆₄–⁷⁄₃₂in

Bearings
Cone and roller	24780
Differential side	Timken
Cup	24721
Shims	
	0.003in, 0.005in, 0.010in, 0.030in
Pinion shaft	Timken
Cone and roller	
	Front 31593 rear 02872
Cup	Front 31520 rear 02820
Shims	
	0.003in, 0.005in, 0.010in, 0.030in
Wheel hub	Timken
Cone and roller	
	Inner 18590 outer 18590
Cup	Inner 18520 outer 18520
Steering knuckle	Timken
Cone and roller	
	Upper 11590 lower 11590
Cup	Upper 11520 lower 11520
Steering bell crank	
Bearing	Needle Torrington B1210

Rear Axle
Type	Full floating
Make	Spicer
Drive	Through springs
Road clearance	8⁷⁄₁₆in

Differential
Drive	Hypoid
Gear ratio	4.88:1
Bearings	Timken roller
Gears (pinion)	2
Oil capacity	2½ US pt
Adjustment	Shims
	0.003in, 0.005in, 0.010in, 0.030in

Pinion shaft
Bearings	Two Timken rollers
Adjustment	Shims

0.003in, 0.005in, 0.010in, 0.030in

Bevel and pinion gear

Backlash	0.005–0.007in
Adjustment	Shims

0.003in, 0.005in, 0.010in, 0.030in

Bearings

Make–differential side	Timken
Cone and roller	24780
Cup	24721
Make–pinion shaft	Timken
Cone and roller	
	Front 02872; rear 31593
Cup	Front 02820; rear 31520
Shims	

0.003in, 0.005in, 0.010in, 0.030in

Make–wheel hub	Timken
Cone and roller	
	Inner 18590; outer 18590
Cup	Inner 18520; outer 18520

Wheel cylinder spring

Length	1⁷⁄₁₆in
Load when compressed	1–1¼lb

Wheels

Make	Kelsey-Hayes
Rim	16 × 4.00 drop centre
	or 16 × 4.50 combat
Tyres	16 × 6.00
Type	Mud and snow non-directional
	tread or highway type tread
Tyre pressures	30–35psi
Bearings – F and R	Inner; outer
Make	Timken; Timken
Cone and roller	18590; 18590
Cup	18520; 18520

Brakes

Service brakes

Type	4-wheel hydraulic
Size	9.0in × 1¾in
Fluid capacity	¾ US pt

Master cylinder

Size	1.0in
Mounted	LH frame side rail

Wheel cylinder

Size	Front 1.0in; rear ¾in

Brake shoes

	Bendix
Size	9 × 1¾in
Lining area	117.8sq in
Length lining-forward shoe	10⁷⁄₃₂in
Length lining-reverse shoe	6³⁹⁄₆₄in
Width	1¾in
Thickness	³⁄₁₆in

Handbrake

Type	Mechanical
Size	6in
Lining	Woven
Length	18⁹⁄₁₆in
Width	2in
Thickness	⁵⁄₃₂in

Brake return springs

Brake pedal	
Free length	5⁷⁄₈in
Load when extended to 7⁹⁄₁₆in	23lb

Brake shoe return spring

Free length	5¹³⁄₁₆in
Load when extended to 6³⁄₁₆in	40lb

Springs

Front spring

Make	Mather
Type, leaf	Parabolic
Length centre-to-centre of eye	36¼in
Width	1¾in
Number of leaves	8
Rebound clips	4
Front eye centre-to-centre bolt	18⅛in
Rear eye centre-to-centre bolt	18⅛in
Left camber under 525lb	⁵⁄₁₆in
Right camber under 390lb	⁵⁄₁₆in
Rear eye bushed	
Bushing size 1¾in long; ID 0.5655in	

Rear spring

Make	Mather
Type, leaf	Parabolic
Length	42in
Width	1¾in
Number of leaves	9
Rebound clips	4
Camber under 800lb	¼in
Eye to centre bolt	21in
Front eye bushed	
	1¾in long ID 0.5655in

Shock Absorbers

Make	Front–	Rear–
	Monroe	Monroe

Type	Hydraulic	Hydraulic
Action	Double	Double
Length compressed	10⁹⁄₁₆in	11⁹⁄₁₆in
Length extended	16⅛in	18⅛in
Adjustable	Yes	Yes
Mountings	Rubber	Rubber

Frame

Frame

Frame		SAE 1025
Depth, maximum		4.186in
Thickness, maximum		0.093in
Flange width		1¾in
Length		122¾in
Width		
Front		29¼in
Rear		29¼in
Number cross members		
	5:– 'K' member at rear	
Weight		140lb

Wheel base 80in

Track (tread)

Front
48¼in – with combat wheels 49in

Rear
48¼in – with combat wheels 49in

Electrical System

Battery

Make	Auto-Lite or Willard
Model	TS-2-15 or SW-2-119
Plates per cell	15
Capacity	116Ah
Voltage	6V
Length, approx	10in
Width, approx	7in
Height, approx	8⁵⁄₁₆in
Specific gravity	
Fully charged	1.225–1.1300
Recharge at	1.175
Earth (ground) terminal	Negative
Location	Under bonnet, right side

Starter motor

Make	Auto-Lite
Model	MZ-4113
Drive	Right-hand outboard Bendix
No-load draw	
	70A max; 5.5V – 4300rpm

Stall torque	420A, 3.0V – 7.8ft lb
Voltage	6V
Armature end play, max	¹⁄₁₆in
Brushes	4
Brush spring tension	42–53oz
Normal engine cranking speed	185rpm
Bearings	3 absorbent bronze

Starter switch

Make	Auto-Lite
Model	SW-4001

Generator

Make	Auto-Lite
Model	GEG-5002D
Voltage	6–8V
Ground polarity	Negative
Controlled output	40A
Rotation (drive end)	Clockwise
Control vibrating type CV regulator	
Air cooled	Yes
Armature end play, max	0.010in
Brushes	2
Brush spring tension	64–8oz
Bearings	Ball
Field coil draw	1.60 to 1.78A 6.00V
Motorising draw	4.7 to 5.2A 6.0V

(Have field and armature terminals connected)

Output	8.0A;	7.6V; 955	max rpm
	40.0A;	7.6V; 1460	max rpm
	40.0A;	8.0V; 1465	max rpm

Constant-voltage regulator

Make	Auto-Lite
Model	VRY-4203A
Voltage	6V
Current	40A
Ground (Earth) polarity	Negative

Voltage regulator

Voltage setting, open circuit	7.20–41
Air gap	0.040–0.042in
Point gap	0.010–0.012in

Circuit breaker

Points closed (hot)	6.4–6.6V
Points open – Reverse current	
	0.5–6.0A
Air gap	0.0595–0.0625in
Points gap	0.015in

Current limiting regulator

Air gap	0.047–0.049in
Point gap	0.030–0.033in

Coupling socket plug

Make	Wagner
Socket model	No 3604

Plug model   No 3744
Distributor
Make   Auto-Lite
Model   IGC-4705
Type advance   Centrifugal
Firing order   1-3-4-2
Breaker point gap   0.020in
Breaker arm spring tension   17–20oz
Cam angle (time points are closed)
                                        47deg
Max automatic advance 1500rpm (dist)
                                        11deg
Condenser capacity   18-26 Mfd
Timing–72 octane fuel (gasoline)
    5deg BTC flywheel (0.0103in piston
                                        travel)
Timing–68 octane fuel (gasoline)
    TC flywheel (zero piston travel)
Timing mark   Flywheel
Location
    Right side bell housing under starter
Ignition switch (lock) Douglas No 5941
Coil
Make   Auto-Lite
Model   IG-4070-L
Draw engine stopped   5A at 6.4V
Draw engine idling   2.5A
Gauges
Fuel gauge   Auto-Lite
Oil pressure   Auto-Lite
Temperature   Auto-Lite
Ammeter   Auto-Lite
Spark plugs
Make   Champion QM-2
Size   14mm
Gap   0.030in
Radio filters
Generator filter unit   Solar SJ-194
                                        Sprague JX-130
            Tobe Deutschmann SC-33M-1
Regulator filter   Solar EV-101
                                        Sprague JX-112
            Tobe Deutschmann 1126
Filter group   Solar EV-103
                                        Sprague JX-17
            Tobe Deutschmann 1107DE
Lamps
Light switch   Douglas
Foot beam switch   Clum No 9654
Headlamps
            Corcoran-Brown sealed beam
Black-out lamps   Corcoran-Brown

Tail and stop lamps   Corcoran-Brown
Headlamp bulbs (Seelite unit)
    6–8V 45CP DC Mazda No 2400
Black-out bulbs
    6–8V 3CP SC Mazda No 63
Tail and stop-lamp bulbs
    6–8V 3-21CP Mazda No 1154
Instrument-lamp bulbs
    6–8V 3CP SC Mazda No 63

Bonded (Earthing) Points

Bond
No   Name
1   Bonnet to dash, right hand
2   Bonnet to dash, left hand
3   Cylinder head stud to dash
4   Brake Cable, speedometer cable,
    heat indicator cable to dash
5   Gas line to dash
6   Choke control, throttle control and
    oil gauge line to dash stud
7   Generator mounting bolt to starting
    motor bracket
8   Generator voltage regulator filter
    and earth (ground)
9   Coil to cylinder block
10 Right-hand front motor bracket to
    frame
11 Left-hand front motor bracket to
    frame
12 Exhaust pipe to frame
13 Radiator right hand to frame
14 Radiator left hand to frame
15 Rear engine support to frame cross
    member stud
16 Transfer case to body floor stud
17 Right-hand body bracket earth to
    frame
18 Left-hand body bracket earth to
    frame
19 Right-hand wing earth to frame
20 Left-hand wing earth to frame
21 Left-hand bonnet earth to grill
22 Right-hand bonnet earth to grill
23 Headlamp wiring harness to left
    wing (fender)
24 Cylinder head stud-front
25 Left-hand wing to cowl, lower
26 Right-hand wing to cowl, lower
Important: Where parts are earthed,
particular attention must be given to any
special positions of lockwashers on bolts
and screws. Tinned spots should be clean
but not painted, to bond properly.

ACKNOWLEDGEMENTS

I cannot list my helpers in alphabetical order because many assisted me in their individual capacity whilst others did so as representatives of organisations. Therefore this tribute to their help is 'out of the hat'. First I thank W. (Bill) S. Pickett, President and General Manager of American Motors (Canada) Ltd, one of the remaining engineers of Willys-Overland, who found time to see me in Brampton, Ontario. The other two AMC people I should like to thank for their co-operation are Ben Dunn and Al Goldberg. Bart Vanderveen of the Olyslager Organisation was equally co-operative.

Ingrid McAllister and her colleagues in the Science and Technology Department of the Metropolitan Reference Library in Toronto were most helpful; I met a similar willingness amongst the staff of the library of the Imperial War Museum in London.

Autocar magazine supplied me with the cutaway Jeep drawing (done as only my friend, the late Max Millar, could have done it), copies of road-test reports on Jeeps and published my Jeep-information enquiry in their correspondence columns. I also want to thank Ron Easton, their chief photographer.

Peter Roberts and Michael Worthington-Williams (head of the Department of Veteran and Special Interest Vehicles at Sotheby Parke Bernet & Co) gave me copies of Jeep material from their collections; of particular value here was a feature by Paul Hackenburg on Harold Crist, chief engineer of Bantam Cars and a true Jeep pioneer.

Anthony P. Bamford, Chairman and MD of J. C. Bamford Ltd (JCB) helped me with information and illustrations, and Michael Turner, best known as a car artist, loaned his own restored MB for use in photographs by Ron Easton.

Malik Idris Khan informed me on the activities of Jeeps in Pakistan, having himself used them for years on his ranch-*cum*-nature reserve. Bernard Venners enlarged on the work of the Military Vehicle Conservation Group (UK) and gave information and illustrations on the restoration work of Mike Priscott. Joe Lyndhurst – who founded the Warnham War Museum near Horsham as a result of his enthusiasm for Jeep restoration – was another who obligingly imparted his knowledge to me. In Bellingham, Washington state, John

Hendricks showed me round his stockpile of spares and enabled me to see the effect of his know-how on Jeep restoration. My friend, Richard Evans – local champion Jeep-modelmaker – also helped me to a better understanding of the subtleties of restoration. Art Volpe, of the Department of the Army (Tank-Automotive Command), Warren, Michigan, supplied details of the specifications to which the military Jeep's successor – the 'Humvee' – must conform.

I'd like to single-out three books which I found particularly useful. They are: *The Jeep* by Bart Vanderveen (Frederick Warne & Co Ltd, 1970, 1975, 1981), *Hail to the Jeep!* by A. W. Wade (Harper & Brothers, 1946) and the *Complete Encyclopaedia of Motor Cars* edited by G. N. Georgano (National Magazine Co, 1973).

Special mention must be made of my wife, Catherine, who slogged through the research with me.

Finally, I know that I have left many people out of this list but the line has to be drawn somewhere. Thank you all.

Michael Clayton, 1982

INDEX

Page references in *italic* type refer to illustrations